GEOGRAPHY BEE
Simplified

GEOGRAPHY BEE

Simplified

A PREPARATION
GUIDE
FOR THE
SCHOOL AND STATE
GEOGRAPHY BEES

SECOND EDITION

Ram Iyer

EDITED BY
Smitha Gundavajhala

Table of Contents

Preface to the Second Edition

Why this guide?

After the successful launch of my first guide, Geography Bee Simplified, as a preparatory guide to my second advanced book, Geography Bee Demystified, there have been some changes around the world. Geography Bee Simplified - Second Edition, incorporates those changes and makes the guide as compatible as possible to the current world. As before, Geography Bee Demystified, is targeted towards advanced students in the State and the National Geographic Bees. This guide, on the other hand, is targeted towards a serious youngster in the 4th, 5th or 6th grades who strives to reach the top. At the same time, there are enough challenging questions that would be very useful even at the state or the national levels if one reframes the questions and take out some of the obvious clues. This guide's main focus is on the National Geographic Society's School Bee, the State Qualifying Test, and the preliminaries and the Final rounds of the State Geography Bee. Many readers appreciated the fact that the guide does not elaborate upon the various stages of the competition that are available free from the National Geographic Society's website or from your school teachers. Instead, this guide gives advice about how to perform in the competitions and gets to the meat of the questions right away.

Who is this guide for?

This guide is for serious contestants. It is for those who already have mastered the basic facts from their previous years and who have a good shot at advancing to the higher levels at their school competitions. At the same time, participants in the State Bee and the National Bee would benefit immensely from using this guide. It is not inconceivable to see some of the questions appear in the advanced rounds of the State Bee and the preliminary rounds of the National Bee as well.

How is the guide organized?

Geography Bee Simplified is divided into twelve chapters. There are seven chapters based primarily on the continents of the world. There are some adjustments, as in the case of a transcontinental country like Russia, which is included under the chapter "Asia." Central American and Caribbean countries are included under "North America." As in the First Edition, there is a separate chapter devoted to Physical Geography. I have added several new questions in this chapter. I have also added two new chapters. They are devoted to Cultural and Economic Geography respectively. This is followed by a short chapter that gives you a taste for advanced-level questions. The question-and-answer format lends itself to an easier way of preparation for those who have limited time to prepare for the geography bee. Crossword puzzles at the end of the chapters add to the fun of learning.

At the end of the guide, there is a chapter exclusively focusing on a sample School/State Geography Bee competition to test the contestant. Ideally, I would ask parents, older siblings, or friends of the contestant to administer this mock bee.

I have added some questions from previous users of my guides. This includes Stefan Petrovic, the 2011 National Geographic Bee third-place winner; Luke Hellum, the 2011 National Geographic Bee seventh-place rank holder; Arjun Kandaswamy, the 2009 National Geographic Bee second-place winner; Zaroug Jaleel, the 2009 National Geographic Top-Ten Finalist; and Spencer Seballos, the 2008 Ohio State second-place winner.

How do I use this guide?

This guide is most useful with the companionship of a good atlas, such as those published by the National Geographic Society, Dorling Kindersley Publishing, and Kingfisher Publishing. You can see the reference section to get more details. Don't forget to look at the wealth of information available at:

http://www.mywonderfulworld.org/

http://www.nationalgeographic.com/geobee/

Take the daily GeoBee Challenge from the National Geographic website every day and make a note of all the questions that are difficult. The resources are free and are informative. Use this guide in conjunction with these resources. To do well, you may need to use multiple resources.

Some helpful hints...

The geography bee competition format is not set in stone. In fact, changes in formats do happen without advance notice. However, based on my close personal experience with previous competitions, I would like to address some of the questions that readers may have in mind and offer some helpful hints.

Are questions in this guide from various competitions conducted by the National Geographic Society?

The answer is "no." Although the guide is written to help prepare for the competitions, using the exact questions from the competitions not only is unethical but would also defeat the very purpose behind the National Geographic Society's competitions. The goal of the National Geographic Society is to increase geography awareness around the country. The competition does not lend itself to a "cramming" session. Instead, it seeks to develop an appreciation of geography. If you have had some experience listening to many of the questions asked, you will realize that the wealth of information delivered through these questions is probably more educational than the question being asked. For example, you will rarely find a question that merely asks," What is the capital of Germany?" Instead, what you will hear is a wealth of information about Berlin delivered in the question in the competition. In keeping with that spirit, I have done my best to avoid questions that resemble what I have already seen or heard. If there are similarities to some of the questions from past competitions, it is purely a coincidence.

How do I prepare? I have other classes, I have a busy schedule at school, and my parents work late.

This is a fact of life. In fact, for most students, the end of the school semester coincides with the School Bee competitions. The earlier you prepare the better. This guide has been written with a view to give participants, under these conditions, some help in developing a game plan. For a school bee, however, paying attention in your classes does most of the job. It is not a bad idea to have a simple atlas and a globe at home and find time to spend 15 minutes or 30 minutes a day on preparation for the geography bee. A few extra hours during the weekend also helps. One can start by referring to Children's Atlases that are available in the market several months before the competitions start. The local library is a great resource. In addition, use this guide to supplement your knowledge and to develop a knack for answering questions and filtering out data from questions that may appear confusing. It is not uncommon to find extraneous data added to a question that could confuse a student. If you learn how to focus on the clues and get to the real question, you are half-way there. To get the best out of this guide, you have to be ready with your atlas and physically locate the answer to each question on the map, and then try to read more about it. As you locate a place, try to see what is around that location. Often times, questions in these competitions tend to use the surrounding places or physical terrain in the adjacent areas as hints. Very seldom will you find a question stated exactly as what you find in the books you have. In other words, you have to know your geography, not just the answers. It is not, however, too complex. The National Geographic Society competitions do not test contestants on trivia. They are about places you often hear but did not realize their importance. There are no trick questions.

How do I prepare for the physical geography questions?

Read your junior high text books. Pay attention to the items you read in 3rd grade. Most teachers would be helpful in lending you a book or two. Do not hesitate to make a visit to your public library. Get books targeted towards 4th, 5th, and 6th graders. Questions in the School Bee and the State Bee tend to be straightforward and may even include multiple choices. Look at some of the questions in the guide and then develop your own questions based on your Earth Science text book.

How do I prepare for the current affairs category?

In this category, questions are formulated with several geography hints. Be aware that fourth graders might be competing with eighth graders, and the personnel in charge of making questions will not be unfair to the fourth graders. One has to be aware of important news items from the past few months but there is no need to fret about what happened on the day before your school bee. Questions are set in advance, in a forty-five day window of the competition. Another important thing to note is the fact that you do not need to remember hard-to-pronounce names of people and places. Yes, the questions could have confusing information. To repeat, develop the skills to focus on the geographic clue in that question. Do the questions specify clues that include borders, a major mountain, a river, or an ocean? Invariably, they do.

What did the pronouncer say?

Let's face it—it's virtually impossible for the pronouncer to pronounce a name in another language as clearly as a native would. What should you do if you are not sure what you heard? Use your quota of repeats. Do not, however, waste your repository of repeats by asking the announcer merely to repeat the question. Often, you did hear the question right the first time! Instead, ask the pronouncer to spell it. You may be surprised to find that you had known the answer all along.

Use your allotted time.

You have 15 seconds to answer a question. Use it. Do not answer a question immediately after it is read—wait until you are in the seventh second. The same concept applies to the State Bee Qualifying test. If you finish the written test early, read your answers again. In populous states like California and New York, this could be critical. There are no bonus points for finishing early.

Disclaimer

The information provided in this guide is based on my own research and that of several geography enthusiasts and competitors. Over the past couple of years, I was fortunate to have the help of a young editor, Smitha Gundavajhala, who is a strong geography student and has participated in competitions at the State level. I was also fortunate to have the help of other participants like Gentry Clark, Anirudh Kumar, and Omkar Shende. Despite input from several bright students, the guide is not guaranteed to be without inaccuracies. Answers may be subject to interpretation and/or reliable sources could offer different data. As you use this guide if you find any errors, please bring them to my attention so that future editions and subsequent versions can be improved. (Please state your sources when you send a correction.)

Please visit http://www.geographybee-coaching.com/ to send your suggestions or corrections. This site may also have new announcements, updates, corrections, and new quizzes.

Acknowledgments

I would like to thank my family, friends, past and current participants, and their parents for having played a major part in motivating me to write the first edition of this study guide and a subsequent second edition. I would also like to thank Smitha Gundavajhala who helped me edit this guide and provide valuable input and suggestions when needed. My interactions with some of the current participants continue to be a motivating factor as well. I want to extend my special thanks to geo-whiz Gentry Clark, the two-time Texas State top-three finalist; Anirudh Kumar, the three-time California State Bee participant; and Omkar Shende, the 2009 second-place winner of the Michigan State Geographic Bee for sharing their experiences. As in the case of my first guide, Smitha Gundavajhala was always able to improve the guide with her own knowledge on the subject matter. I also want to thank my own boys, Suneil and Eswar, who were willing to help out when their schedules permitted. I take pride in the fact that both the guides received help from all the competitors from the past and the present who have helped enhance the quality of the guide. Not all competitors who helped me are rank-holders, but they all have a passion for the subject and are as competent as anyone else.

Chapter 1

The United States

1. Which U.S. capital city, a trade center for agricultural products from Idaho and eastern Oregon, is home to the only Basque Museum in the United States?
    Boise

2. Name the U.S. state that is dominated by the Bitterroot Range along its border with Montana and is drained chiefly by the Snake River.
    Idaho

3. Name the capital city of the U.S. state located to the south of Wisconsin and bordered by Kentucky and Missouri.
    Springfield

4. The Sears Tower and the Shedd Aquarium are popular tourist sites in Illinois's "Windy City." Name this city.
    Chicago

5. The Lincoln Boyhood National Memorial and George Rogers Clark National Historic Park are major landmarks in which state bordering Illinois and Ohio?
    Indiana

6. Which U.S. state is located between the Missouri and Mississippi Rivers and borders Wisconsin and South Dakota?
    Iowa

7. Name the Midwestern U.S. city situated near the confluence of the Raccoon River and a river of the same name as the city.
    Des Moines

8. Dodge City, the cowboy capital, is an important tourist attraction in which U.S. state that is one of the leading producers of wheat in the nation?
    Kansas

9. Indiana's largest city, home to the Motor Speedway, is situated on the White River. Name this city.
Indianapolis

10. Which city in Illinois is well-known for a major fire in 1871 that destroyed most of its wooden buildings?
Chicago

11. Which is Missouri's largest city—Kansas City or St. Louis?
Kansas City

12. The Tallgrass Prairie National Preserve contains the largest expanse of Tallgrass prairie in the United States. This is in which U.S. state?
Kansas

13. Mammoth Cave National Park and the Abraham Lincoln Birthplace National Historic Site are major tourist attractions in the Bluegrass state. Name this state.
Kentucky

14. The capital city of a U.S. state bordering Michigan and Minnesota is situated on an isthmus between Lake Mendota and Lake Monona. Name this city.
Madison

15. What city, near the confluence of the Coosa and Tallapoosa rivers, became the first capital of the Confederate States of America?
Montgomery

16. The northern part of Alabama has rich deposits of coal and iron ore. This area lies along what mountains?
Appalachian Mountains

17. What capital city, named after President Andrew Jackson, is located on the Pearl River?
Jackson

18. In the 1960s, the civil rights movement began in Montgomery and Birmingham in what U.S. state?
Alabama

19. The Tombigbee River and what other river form the chief river system of Alabama?
The Tennessee River

20. Because the Aleutian Islands extend beyond the 180th meridian, the northernmost and the westernmost U.S. state could also be considered as the easternmost. Name this state.
Alaska

21. Which is the largest city in Kansas—Kansas City or Wichita?
Wichita

22. Washington Island lies to the northeast of the Door Peninsula in which state?
Wisconsin

23. What strait separates Alaska from Russia?
The Bering Strait

24. What U.S. state has a longer coastline than any other state?
Alaska

25. Juneau, Alaska's chief seaport and capital, is situated on what channel?
Gatineau Channel

26. The Apostle Islands National Lakeshore and the National Railroad Museum are important destinations for tourists visiting what state bordering Lake Superior and the state of Minnesota?
Wisconsin

27. Name the largest U.S. state by area.
Alaska

28. Name the U.S. state that has both the Coast Range and the Brooks Range.
Alaska

29. On the Alaskan flag, the stars in the Big Dipper signify what mineral resource?
Gold

30. The reconstructed London Bridge can be found in Lake Havasu City in what southwestern state bordering Mexico?
Arizona

31. What plateau occupies the northern part of Arizona?
The Colorado Plateau

32. Arizona's capital city was founded in 1870 on the Salt River. Name this city.
Phoenix

33. The United States gained most of the territory in Arizona after what war fought between 1846 and 1848?
The Mexican War

34. Arkansas is bounded by what river to its east?
Mississippi

35. Arkansas is the only U.S. state that produces what precious gem?
Diamond

36. The Ozark Plateau and what mountains meet the plains near Arkansas' capital city of Little Rock?
Ouachita Mountains

37. Little Rock was founded in 1814 on the banks of what river?
The Arkansas River

38. Which state does not border Arkansas—Tennessee or Kansas?
Kansas

39. San Joaquin River is one of the rivers flows in Central Valley between the coastal ranges and the Sierra Nevada Mountains in what U.S. state?
California

40. Death Valley and what other desert occupy California's southeast region?
Mojave Desert

41. With an average elevation of 6,800 ft, which is the highest state in the U.S.—Colorado or Alaska?
Colorado

42. The Mesa Verde National Park is an important tourist site in Colorado near its border with Utah, Arizona, and what other state?
New Mexico

43. Colorado's capital city is nicknamed as the "Mile High City." Name this city.
Denver

44. Pikes Peak lies to the west of which major city in Colorado?
Colorado Springs

45. Name Colorado's highest peak located on the Sawatch Range.
Mt. Elbert

46. Which state does not border Colorado—Oklahoma or Iowa?
Iowa

47. In 1623, Dutch Settlers founded what major city on the Connecticut River?
Hartford

48. Mystic Seaport, once a major shipyard, is now an important tourist site in what state on the Long Island Sound?
Connecticut

49. Name the state that has Birmingham as its largest city that used to be a major center of cotton industry before the Civil War.
Alabama

50. The Central Valley Project is the largest water transfer that feeds the San Joaquin and Sacramento Valleys in which U.S. state?
California

51. Which Floridian city is sometimes known as the bilingual gateway for Latin America?
Miami

52. Name New England's longest waterway.
The Connecticut River

53. Eli Whitney and Samuel Colt once had major firearms manufacturing centers in what state bordering New York to its west?
Connecticut

54. Name the second smallest state by area.
Delaware

55. The Delaware River is an important shipping route through which city in Pennsylvania?
Philadelphia

56. Lake Okeechobee is the biggest lake in the southern United States. This is in what state that was purchased by United States from Spain in 1819?
Florida

57. Name Florida's largest wetland.
The Everglades

58. In 1539, which city in Florida was the site of a Spanish mission and was considered to be the first European discovery?
Tallahassee

59. Georgia's capital city was formerly known as Marthasville in 1843 and Terminus in the early 1800s. Name this city.
Atlanta

60. The McClellan Air Base is located near what inland port in Central California?
Sacramento

61. The Confederate Memorial at Stone Mountain is an important historic site in what U.S. state bordering Alabama and South Carolina?
Georgia

62. The mouth of the Altamaha River in Georgia is in what body of water?
The Atlantic Ocean

63. Kilauea, the most active volcano on Earth, is on the largest island in Hawaii. Name this island.
Hawaii (Big Island)

64. Honolulu is on what Hawaiian island?
Oahu

65. Among Hawaii's most important economic activities are tourism, sugar refining, and the canning of a fruit that made the state famous. Name this fruit.
Pineapple

66. North America's highest peak Mt. McKinley is in Alaska, Mt. McKinley is also known by what name?
Denali

67. America's largest national forest is in the state of Alaska. Name this national forest.
The Tongass National Forest

68. The Trans-Alaska Pipeline carries oil from what town on the Beaufort Sea to Valdez on the Gulf of Alaska?
Prudhoe Bay

69. Name New Hampshire's southernmost largest city on Merrimack River.
Nashua

70. What river forms New Hampshire's border with Vermont?
Connecticut River

71. Mt. Washington is the tallest peak in what mountains?
The White Mountains

72. One of the first warships of the American navy was built at Portsmouth in 1776. Portsmouth lies closest to New Hampshire's border with what state?
Maine

73. In 1776, George Washington crossed what river to defeat Hessian troops during the Revolutionary war?
The Delaware River

74. In 1620, the Dutch founded the colony of New Netherland which is now known by what name?
New York

75. In 1664, the British acquired the territory of New Netherland and created New Jersey when they separated the land between the Delaware and what other river?
The Hudson River

76. The Kittatinny Mountains are located in the Pennsylvania, New York and what other state?
New Jersey

77. What U.S. state capital was founded at the foot of the Sangre de Cristo Mountains and is regarded as the oldest capital city in the U.S?
Santa Fe

78. The San Juan Mountains run through Colorado and the "Land of Enchantment." Name this state.
New Mexico

79. In 1524, Giovanni da Verrazano discovered what island in the Empire state?
Manhattan Island

80. The Mohawk River, an important river in New York, is the tributary of what major river?
The Hudson River

81. The opening of a major canal propelled New York's growth in 1825. Name this canal.
The Erie Canal

82. Buffalo, New York, is on what lake—Lake Erie or Lake Ontario?
Lake Erie

83. Oswego, New York, is on what lake?
Lake Ontario

84. Name the largest city on New York's Genesee River.
Rochester

85. The Research Triangle in North Carolina comprises Durham, Raleigh, and which city?
Chapel Hill

86. Which U.S. state is the leading producer of tobacco?
North Carolina

87. The Edison National Historic Site and the Morristown National Historic Park are important landmarks in what state that borders Delaware and New York?
New Jersey

88. Name the U.S. state that was nicknamed the Sandwich Islands by Captain James Cook.
Hawaii

89. Following the onslaught of the General William Sherman's Army in 1864, which Atlantic U.S. state bordering North Carolina and Florida was readmitted to the Union in 1870?
Georgia

90. The Appalachian Mountains run across North Carolina's border with which state to Kentucky's south?
Tennessee

91. What river drains into the Albemarle Sound in North Carolina?
The Roanoke River

92. Name the principal mountain range in the southeast region of the state of New York.
The Catskills

93. The Carlsbad Caverns National Park and Chaco Culture National Historic Park are tourist attractions in what state bordering Arizona and Oklahoma?
New Mexico

94. Name the principal mountain range in the northeast region of the state of New York.
The Adirondacks

95. The headquarters of Coca-Cola and the Emory University are located in which city in Georgia?
Atlanta

96. Grand Forks is a large city across Minnesota's border in what state?
North Dakota

97. Mount Waialeale, considered by some to be the wettest place on Earth, is in which U.S. state separated from continental United States by about 2,400 miles of ocean.
Hawaii

98. North Dakota's capital is situated on the Missouri River. Name this city.
Bismarck

99. What harbor is the site of the USS Arizona Memorial on the island of Oahu?
Pearl Harbor

100. In 1874, discovery of what mineral led to an increase in population in the Black Hills of South Dakota. Name this mineral.
Gold

101. Name the only Confederate capital city east of the Mississippi River that was not captured by the Union Army.
Tallahassee

102. Pierre, South Dakota, is on what river?
The Missouri River

103. Which U.S. state produces the largest amount of gold?
Nevada

104. What U.S. capital city lies on the Scioto River?
Columbus

105. The Rock and Roll Hall of Fame is an attraction in the Buckeye state. Name this state.
Ohio

106. Sandusky, Ohio, is located on what large body of water?
Lake Erie

107. The Iolani Palace is the only royal residence on U.S. soil. This is in the youngest state in the union. Name this state.
Hawaii

108. Dayton, Ohio, lies on what river?
The Great Miami River

109. The Football Hall of Fame is in Canton in what state bordering West Virginia and Indiana?
Ohio

110. Toledo, Ohio lies closest to what bordering state?
Michigan

111. The Outer Banks and Cape Hatteras are tourist attractions in the Tar Heel state. Name this state.
North Carolina

112. The Will Rogers Home and Memorial, and the Chickasaw National Recreation Area are attractions in the Sooner State. Name this state.
Oklahoma

113. Oklahoma City is located on what river?
The North Canadian River

114. The Red River forms Oklahoma's southern border with the Lone Star State. Name this state.
Texas

115. Black Mesa is situated in the western panhandle region of what state bordering Colorado, New Mexico, and Texas?
Oklahoma

116. Name the state that forms Oklahoma's shortest border to its east.
Missouri

117. The founding of a Franciscan mission in 1769 was the first
European settlement in California. This was in which large city
not far from the Mexican border?
San Diego

118. Oregon's Willamette Valley lies between the Cascade Range and
which mountain range that runs parallel to the Pacific Ocean?
Coast Mountains

119. Name Oregon's highest peak in the Cascade Ranges.
Mount Hood

120. What river forms the boundary between Washington and
Oregon?
The Columbia River

121. The Columbia plateau separates Oregon from which state to its
east?
Idaho

122. In 1848, gold was discovered at Sutter's Mill in what U.S. state?
California

123. The Crater Lake National Park and the John Day Fossil Beds attractions are in which northwestern state that has Salem as its
capital city?
Oregon

124. The Valley Forge National Historic Park is an important historic
site in "The City of Brotherly Love" in Pennsylvania. Name
this city.
Philadelphia

125. The Badlands is a magnificent feature in the western part of the Flickertail State. Name this state.
North Dakota

126. In 1979, a major nuclear disaster was barely avoided in which power station in Pennsylvania?
Three Mile Island

127. Name the city in Pennsylvania that is well-known for its chocolate production.
Hershey

128. The U.S. state capital of Harrisburg is situated on what river?
The Susquehanna River

129. Prudence Island, Conanicut Island, and Block Island belong to which U.S. state?
Rhode Island

130. The opening shots of the Civil War were fired at Fort Sumter in what state south of North Carolina?
South Carolina

131. Name the U.S. state capital at the junction of the Broad, Saluda and Congaree Rivers.
Columbia

132. Myrtle Beach and Hilton Head are important tourist attractions in which U.S. state?
South Carolina

133. The National Cowboy Hall of Fame is located near which U.S. capital city?
Oklahoma City

134. A state capital on the Cumberland River is home of the Country Music Hall of Fame. Name this city.
Nashville

135. Chattanooga and Shiloh were major battle sites in what state that is nicknamed the "Volunteer State?"
Tennessee

136. Which city in Pennsylvania served as the U.S. capital from 1790 to 1800?
Philadelphia

137. The Battle of Gettysburg was fought in the Keystone State. Name this state.
Pennsylvania

138. The Great Smoky Mountains, running along the eastern border of Tennessee, are part of what larger mountain chain?
The Appalachian Mountains

139. The city of Waterloo was renamed in 1839 to Austin in honor of Stephen Austin. This city lies on what river?
The Colorado River

140. The Llano Estacado is part of an expansive prairie that extends from Texas to which bordering state?
New Mexico

141. The Chisos Mountains are situated near the Big Bend National Park close to Mexico's border with which U.S. state?
Texas

142. The Mandan and Sioux tribes prospered in 1738 before French explorers began their inroads into their territories in what state on the Canadian border?
North Dakota

143. Uinta Mountains and the Dinosaur National Monument are located in the northeastern region of what state bordering Idaho and Colorado?
Utah

144. The Johnson Space Center is located in which Texan city?
Houston

145. The Davis and Guadeloupe Mountains are situated in the western part of what U.S. state that has a coastline on the Gulf of Mexico?
Texas

146. The city of Galveston lies on the coast of what body of water?
Gulf of Mexico

147. Name the U.S. state that holds many of the country's renowned tourist spots, including the Arches, Canyonlands, Zion and the Grand Staircase National Parks.
Utah

148. The city of Langtry, Texas lies near the confluence of the Rio Grande and what river west of the Edward Plateau?
The Pecos River

149. In 1847, Brigham Young founded what city that later became the headquarters of the Mormon Church?
Salt Lake City

150. The Wasatch Range forms a natural border between Utah's mountainous eastern region and what basin that holds the Great Salt Lake?
The Great Basin

151. Glen Canyon and Lake Powell are major tourist destinations for outdoor enthusiasts in which U.S. state bordering Arizona?
Utah

152. What New England state capital lies at the confluence of the Winooski and North Branch Rivers?
Montpelier

153.   Name the largest lake in New England.
Lake Champlain

154.   The Cowpens National Battlefield is important testimony to the military history of what U.S. state that has the Savannah River as part of its border with Georgia?
South Carolina

155.   The Green Mountains dominate what U.S. state bordering New Hampshire and New York?
Vermont

156.   In 1607, the first permanent British settlement in North America was established in which historic city in Virginia?
Jamestown

157.   The historic city of Williamsburg is located in what state bordering Maryland and Tennessee?
Virginia

158.   Fort Vancouver National Historic Site and the North Cascades National Park are important destinations for tourists visiting which northwestern U.S. state?
Washington

159.   The Padre Island National Seashore is an important tourist destination in what U.S. state?
Texas

160.   The Strait of Juan de Fuca and the Strait of Georgia separate Washington from which Canadian island?
Vancouver Island

161.   Name the last state to secede from the Union that also holds the distinction as the first southern state to be readmitted to the Union in 1866.
Tennessee

162. Washington's capital city is located at the Puget Sound. Name this city.
Olympia

163. Mount St. Helens and what other well-known volcano in Washington are an important indicator tectonic activity along the U.S west coast?
Mount Rainier

164. The city of Charleston, at the confluence of the Elk and the Kanawha Rivers, is the capital of the Mountain State. Name this state.
West Virginia

165. West Virginia's eastern panhandle is situated between Virginia and what other state?
Maryland

166. West Virginia's western panhandle is situated between Pennsylvania and what other state?
Ohio

167. What river forms most of the northern border of West Virginia near Maryland?
The Potomac River

168. The historic town of Shepherdstown, West Virginia is located in what mountains, which is part of the larger Appalachian Mountain system?
The Allegheny Mountains

169. Which U.S. state is the leading producer of bituminous coal?
West Virginia

170. What U.S. state capital takes its name from William Trent, a colonial merchant?
Trenton

171. Name the U.S. territory, east of Puerto Rico, which consists of three major islands, St. Thomas, St. John, and St. Croix.
U.S. Virgin Islands

172. The United States military carried out several nuclear tests between 1946 and 1958 on the Pacific islands of Eniwetok and Bikini. These islands belong to what country that is an independent republic in Micronesia?
Marshall Islands

173. The Fort Laramie National Historic Site and the Devil's Tower National Monument are located in which state?
Wyoming

174. The U.S. Anderson Air Force Base is in which U.S. territory?
Guam

175. The historic South Pass helped pioneers in their westward migration. South Pass is in which U.S. state that has the Wind River and the Absaroka Mountain Ranges?
Wyoming

176. In the 1860s, first-time new settlers arrived in Wyoming via Oregon Trail and what other historic trail?
The Bozeman Trail

177. Name Wisconsin's largest city on Lake Michigan.
Milwaukee

178. Wisconsin is the nation's leading producer of what dairy product?
Cheese

179. The National Railroad Museum and the St. Croix National Scenic Railway are tourist highlights in the Badger State. Name this state.
Wisconsin

180. Pago Pago is the capital city of a U.S. territory that has jurisdiction over the Manu'a Islands. Name this Pacific territory.
American Samoa

181. Name the largest U.S. territory by area.
Puerto Rico

182. In 1986, the U.S. government approved the Compact of Free Association with which republic that allowed the U.S. military to use their missile range in the Kwajalein Atoll?
Marshall Islands

183. Name the largest U.S. Pacific territory.
Guam

184. Chamorro and Philippine languages are widely spoken in Guam and what other U.S. Pacific territory?
Northern Mariana Islands

185. Ponce, a major city in Puerto Rico, is on what body of water?
Caribbean Sea

186. The El Yunque National Forest is located in which U.S. territory to the east of Hispaniola?
Puerto Rico

187. The Natchez Trace Parkway is an important landmark in what U.S. state that has Pascagoula as an important coastal city on the Gulf of Mexico?
Mississippi

188. The Mississippi Delta covers almost one quarter of the total area of what state named after the French King Louis XIV?
Louisiana

189. Name the southeastern state whose capital city is on the James River.
Virginia

190. The George Washington Carver Museum is in what state whose southern portion is dominated by the Ozark Plateau?
Missouri

191. The Glacier National Park and the Custer Battlefield National Monument are important attractions in which U.S. state to the east of the Bitterroot Range?
Montana

192. The city of Lancaster, founded in 1856, changed its name in honor of a U.S. President. Name this city that is Nebraska's second-largest city.
Lincoln

193. In 1859, silver was discovered at the Comstock Lode. This discovery propelled which Nevada City situated between Lake Tahoe and the Pine Nut Mountains into prominence?
Carson City (also acceptable: Virginia City)

194. Which U.S. state has the least rainfall?
Nevada

195. The Tennessee-Tombigbee Waterway connects several miles of U.S. inland waterways to the Gulf of Mexico via the port of Mobile in what U.S. state?
Alabama

196. Stamford is an important industrial center in which U.S. state bordering New York and Massachusetts that has one of the highest per capita incomes in the country?
Connecticut

197. Which is not a New England state—New York or Connecticut?
New York

198. The Absaroka Range runs across Montana and which state to its south?
Wyoming

199. Name the state, known for Hot Springs National Park, which is the largest producer of bromine.
Arkansas

200. Which is the largest of the New England states?
Maine

201. Lake Mead is situated at the border of Arizona and which other state?
Nevada

202. The Harry S. Truman National Historic Site and the Ulysses Grant Historic Site draw tourists to which state bordering Arkansas and Iowa?
Missouri

203. The Chimney Rock National Historic Site is an important landmark in which state that contains the confluence of the North Platte and South Platte Rivers?
Nebraska

204. The Laramie Mountains and the Big Horn Mountains are located in what state that has the nation's second largest national park after the Wrangell-St. Elias National Park in Alaska?
Wyoming

205. Which city is more populated—Juneau, Alaska or Montgomery, Alabama?
Montgomery, Alabama

206. San Joaquin Valley is in the most populous state in the U.S. Name this state.
California

207. Aspen and Telluride are important tourist cities in which U.S. state that is nicknamed the Centennial State?
Colorado

208. Name the only U.S. state that borders New Brunswick, Canada.
Maine

209. The nation's largest peanut producer is also a leading supplier of wood pulp. Name this state.
Georgia

210. Which state has a shorter coastline along the Gulf of Mexico—Alabama or Mississippi?
Alabama

211. Mt. Katahdin, the highest point in the Baxter State Park, is in which New England state—New York or Maine?
Maine

212. Name Hawaii's largest ethnic group after the Japanese.
Filipino

213. The Craters of the Moon National Monument is an important site in which U.S. state known for its Hells Canyon, the deepest gorge in the lower 48 states?
Idaho

214. Name the city in Illinois that is linked to the Atlantic by the St. Lawrence Seaway that ships cargo deep into the United States via the Illinois and the Mississippi Rivers.
Chicago

215. The nation's first planned city was laid out in 1733 in Georgia. Name this industrial port city.
Savannah

216. Cadillac Mountain is the highest point in the Acadia National Park along the Atlantic coast of North America. This is in what state to the east of New Hampshire?
Maine

217. Channel Islands belong to which state bordering Arizona and Nevada?
California

218. Egan Range is in the eastern part of what state that borders Idaho and California west of Utah?
Nevada

219. What Georgian city began as a railhead in 1837 before the Civil War?
Atlanta

220. The U.S. Naval Submarine Base is in Groton in what U.S. state bordering Rhode Island and Massachusetts?
Connecticut

221. The panhandle of which state is located south of Alabama?
Florida

222. Where would you find Finger Lakes—New York or Pennsylvania?
New York

223. West Quoddy Head, the easternmost point on mainland United States, is in what state?
Maine

224. Which southern U.S. city holds the famous carnival called the Mardi Gras?
New Orleans

225. Before the railways were built, what inland water route was North America's most important trading route?
The Mississippi River

226. Savannah is a major coastal city in which U.S. state bordering South Carolina and Florida?

Georgia

227. Name all the New England states.
Maine, New Hampshire, Vermont, Massachusetts, Rhode Island, and Connecticut

228. The Apostle Islands National Seashore and the National Railroad Museum are located in which state that has Lake Winnebago as its largest inland lake?
Wisconsin

229. The Yazoo River drains into the Mississippi River in which city?
Vicksburg

230. Washington Island, Wisconsin, is located at the tip of Wisconsin's long, narrow peninsula. Name this peninsula.
The Door Peninsula

231. Martin Luther King, Jr., an African American Nobel Prize winner, was born in what city in Georgia?
Atlanta

232. What river forms Wisconsin's border with Iowa?
The Mississippi River

233. The capital of which northeastern U.S. state is situated on the Merrimack River?
New Hampshire

234. Jefferson City, on the Missouri River, is the capital of which state?
Missouri

235. The Great Smoky Mountains National Park and the Fort Donnellson and Stones River National Battlefields are important sites in what state bordering Alabama and Kentucky?
Tennessee

236. The Pine Mountains, part of the larger Cumberland range, dominate the eastern part of what state that has Frankfort as its capital?
Kentucky

237. Which state capital, a port on the St. Jones River, is located on a peninsula between the Chesapeake Bay and the Delaware Bay?
Dover

238. What sound borders Alabama?
Mississippi Sound

239. A U.S. state, nicknamed the "First State," was the first to pass a coastal-zone act to control waterfront pollution. Name this state.
Delaware

240. The Walt Disney World is an important tourist destination in which Floridian city?
Orlando

241. A chain of small coral islands is the world's third largest reef system, following the Great Barrier Reef and the Belize Reef System. Name this tourist attraction in Florida.
Florida Keys

242. Carlsbad, New Mexico, is situated on what river?
The Pecos River

243. The largest estuary in the United States?
The Chesapeake Bay

244. Name the U.S. state that straddles the Tropic of Cancer.
Hawaii

245. Name the National Park with the largest Mangrove swamp in the continental United States.
Everglades National Park

246.   What mountains occupy most of western Colorado?
Rocky Mountains

247.   Cedar Rapids, Davenport, and Sioux City are major cities in what state?
Iowa

248.   What major city in Arkansas is located on the border of Texas and Arkansas?
Texarkana

249.   Effigy Mounds National Park is located in which state?
Iowa

250.   The John F. Kennedy Space Center is located in what city?
Cape Canaveral

U.S. State Nicknames

ACROSS:

2. The Show Me State
5. The Garden State
6. The Hoosier State
9. The Buckeye State
10. The Volunteer State
11. The Granite State
14. The Sunshine State
15. Natural State
16. The Beehive State
17. The Bay State
18. The Ocean State
19. The Golden State
20. The Sooner State

DOWN:

1. The Keystone State
3. The Prairie State
4. The Beaver State
7. The Palmetto State
8. The North Star State
12. The Sunflower State
13. The Tar Heel State

U.S. State Nicknames

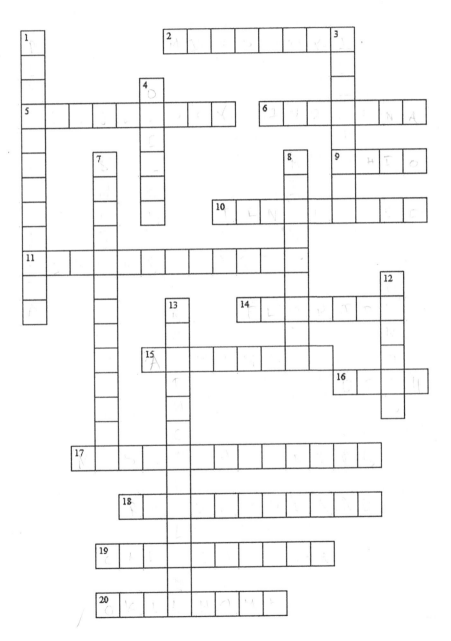

The United States, Part II

ACROSS

5. The Bitterroot Range is shared between Idaho and this other state
6. Kansas City can be found both in Kansas and this other state
10. New York is the only U.S. state to border this Great Lake
12. The Mediterranean climate of this state makes it a major producer of olives and oranges
13. The oldest capital city in the United States
15. The capital of this western state is on the Willamette River
16. The only state in the U.S. that borders the Canadian province of New Brunswick
17. Vancouver is a city both in British Columbia and in this U.S. state that borders it
19. This volcano in Hawaii is the largest in the world

DOWN

1. Ciudad Juarez is to El Paso as Tijuana is to _____
2. This river forms longest stretch of border between Georgia and South Carolina
3. The sea north of Alaska
4. This city is known as "Crescent City" or the "Big Easy"
6. This state consists of mainly two peninsulas
7. The river that forms the border between Texas and Mexico
8. Wake Island is a U.S. territory in this ocean
9. This lake in Minnesota is the source of the Mississippi
11. This state's panhandle borders four other states
14. The first battle to be fought on U.S. soil in World War II was on this Hawaiian island
18. The plateau that spans Arkansas and Missouri

United States - Part II

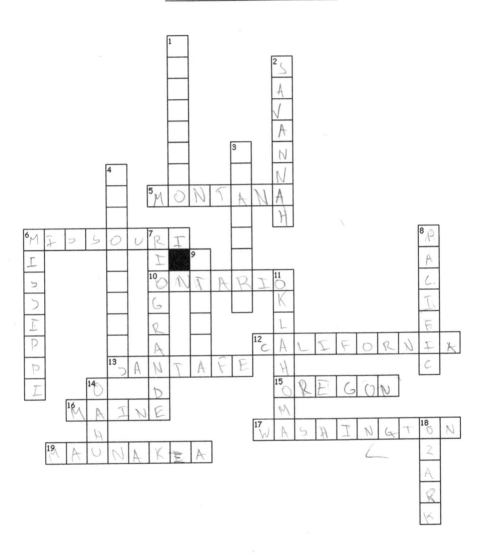

Chapter 2

North America
(including Central America and the Caribbean)

1. The Rio Grande River drains into what body of water?
    Gulf of Mexico

2. Which Mexican state that has Monterrey as its capital has its shortest border with the United States?
    Nuevo Leon

3. Teotihuacan, "the city of the gods," once the capital city of an ancient Mexican civilization, is near which modern city in Mexico?
    Mexico City

4. The modern-day Mexico City is situated on the site of an ancient city that was once the capital of the Aztec civilization. What was the name of that ancient city—Teotihuacan or Tenochtitlan?
    Tenochtitlan

5. Tampico, Mexico lies on the coast of what body of water?
    Gulf of Mexico

6. Tijuana and Mexicali are Mexican cities located on Mexico's border with what country?
    The United States

7. Acapulco is a major tourist attraction on what body of water?
    The Pacific Ocean

8. Name Mexico's largest lake.
    Lake Chapala

9. Cape San Lucas is at the southernmost tip of what Mexican peninsula?
    Baja Peninsula (Baja California)

10. The ruins of Chichen Itza and Uxmal are important sites in which Mexican peninsula?
    Yucatan Peninsula

11. Zócalo, a huge town square, is found in which populous Mexican city?
Mexico City

12. Durango, Mexico lies closest to one of the two major mountain ranges. Name this range.
Sierra Madre Occidental

13. Which famous volcano lies closest to Mexico City—Popocatepetl or Pico de Orizaba?
Popocatepetl

14. San Luis Potosi is a major city in which Latin American country—Bolivia or Mexico?
Mexico

15. The Patuca River is an important river in which Central American country that has Tegucigalpa as its capital?
Honduras

16. The historic city of Copan is situated in what country bordering Guatemala and Nicaragua?
Honduras

17. Name the island country closest to U.S. state of Florida.
Bahamas

18. Volcan Tajamulco, is the highest peak in what country bordering El Salvador and Belize?
Guatemala

19. Bluefields is the largest city on the Mosquito Coast of which country that is the largest in Central America?
Nicaragua

20. Puerto Limon, on the Caribbean Sea, is a major port in what country separated from Nicaragua by the San Juan River?
Costa Rica

21. The Baru Volcano is situated in what country well-known for a major canal linking the Caribbean Sea to the Pacific Ocean?
Panama

22. Belmopan is the capital of Central America's least populous country bordering Mexico and Guatemala. Name this country.
Belize

23. The Coco River forms part of the Honduran border with what country?
Nicaragua

24. Name the Canadian province that extends farthest east.
Newfoundland and Labrador

25. Cape Race, at the southern tip of the Avalon Peninsula, is on what Canadian island?
Newfoundland

26. The Bay of Fundy is situated between which two Canadian provinces?
New Brunswick and Nova Scotia

27. What strait separates Baffin Island from Quebec?
Hudson Strait

28. Name the country in the Americas that has the second largest oil reserves in the world?
Canada

29. The Ellesmere Island belongs to Canada's newest territory. Name this territory that is Canada's largest by area.
Nunavut

30. Name the highest peak in the Canadian portion of the St. Elias Mountains.
   Mt. Logan

31. Uranium City is situated in which province that shares Lake Athabasca with Alberta.
   Saskatchewan

32. Lake Winnipeg is located in which Canadian province?
   Manitoba

33. Churchill, Manitoba lies on what bay?
   Hudson Bay

34. Canada's longest river shares its name with a mountain range that runs from Northwest Territories to Yukon. Name this river.
   The Mackenzie River

35. Canada's largest lake is located in Northwest Territories. Name this lake.
   The Great Bear Lake

36. World's largest freshwater lake is in North America. Name this lake.
   Lake Superior

37. Canada's smallest province, Prince Edward Island, lies on what gulf?
   Gulf of St. Lawrence

38. British Columbia's capital lies at the southern tip of Vancouver Island. Name this city.
   Victoria

39. Alberta's capital lies on the North Saskatchewan River. Name this city.
   Edmonton

40. The city of Windsor is the southernmost city in which Canadian province?
Ontario

41. The Niagara Falls connects Lake Erie with what lake?
Lake Ontario

42. Canada's Horseshoe Falls is situated on what river?
The Niagara River

43. Name the westernmost of the Great Lakes that borders United States and Canada.
Lake Superior

44. Davis Strait separates Baffin Island from what large island?
Greenland

45. The Parry Channel connects Baffin Bay to what sea?
Beaufort Sea

46. Name Canada's deepest lake.
The Great Slave Lake

47. The Ungava Peninsula is in which country on the North American continent?
Canada

48. Nunavut is the youngest political unit in Canada. What is the youngest state in the United States of America?
Hawaii

49. Name the major highway that connects the island of Newfoundland and the Vancouver Island.
The Trans-Canada Highway

50. Which Canadian province extends farthest south?
Ontario

51. Which Canadian territory extends farthest north?
Nunavut

52. Chichen Itza, the pre-Columbian archaeological site on Mexico's Yucatan Peninsula, was built by what civilization?
The Mayan Civilization

53. The Calgary Stampede is a well-known rodeo that takes place every summer in which Canadian province bordering British Columbia and Saskatchewan?
Alberta

54. The Winterlude Festival is held in Canada's capital city. Name this city.
Ottawa

55. Which lies east—Nova Scotia or British Columbia?
Nova Scotia

56. Name the isthmus that links Central America to South America.
Isthmus of Panama

57. Name the major island in the Greater Antilles that extends farthest east.
Puerto Rico

58. Name the largest country on the island of Hispaniola.
The Dominican Republic

59. What island in the Bahamas is considered to be the place where Christopher Columbus anchored in 1492?
San Salvador

60. Name the largest country separated from mainland United States by the Straits of Florida.
Cuba

61. Montego Bay is located in which country that has English as its official language?
Jamaica

62. Name the westernmost capital city in the Greater Antilles?
Havana

63. Name the most populous country in the West Indies.
Cuba

64. The island of Curacao, in the Lesser Antilles, belongs to which country?
Netherlands

65. Name the westernmost island in the Lesser Antilles.
Aruba

66. Name the island, south of Dominica that belongs to France.
Martinique

67. What major island in the Greater Antilles extends farthest west?
Cuba

68. Name the island group in the northeastern Leeward Island chain that has territories belonging to both the United States and the United Kingdom.
Virgin Islands

69. Kingstown is the capital of which country in the Windward Island group?
St. Vincent and the Grenadines

70. The Windward and the Leeward Island chains are part of what larger island group?
Lesser Antilles

71. Cozumel Island belongs to what country?
Mexico

72. Name the U.S. commonwealth that is situated to the east of the island of Hispaniola in the Greater Antilles.
Puerto Rico

73. Baja California belongs to what country—United States or Mexico?
Mexico

74. Lake Nipigon is in which Canadian province?
Ontario

75. In which North American country would you find the Copper Canyon?
Mexico

North American National Parks

ACROSS

1. Pico de Orizaba National Park contains the highest peak in this country.
4. _____ National Park, located in Yukon Territory, is home to Mount Logan.
6. _____ National Park contains the tallest peak in contiguous states.
12. Big Bend National Park, in Texas, is on this river.
15. This national park lies on the site of the Toltecs' ancient capital.
17. Black Canyon of the Gunnison National Park is located in this U.S. State
18. Santa Cruz and Santa Rosa are islands in this National Park.
19. San Lorenzo National Park is found at the mouth of the Chagres River in this country.
20. Banff National Park is located in this Canadian province

DOWN

2. Palenque National Park is in this Mexican state.
3. _____ National Park is nicknamed the "Jewel of the Rockies."
5. _____- St. Elias National Park is the largest in the United States by area.
7. Bruce Peninsula National Park is in this Canadian province.
8. One can find Wapusk National Park in this Canadian province.
9. Name the oldest national park in the United States.
10. Cape Breton Highlands National Park is in this Canadian province
11. The largest national park in Canada.
13. _____ National Park contains the deepest lake in the United States
14. This national park, adjacent to Banff, is on the British Columbia side of the border
16. In Glacier-Waterton National Park, the Waterton half is in Alberta, and the Glacier half is in _____.

North American National Parks

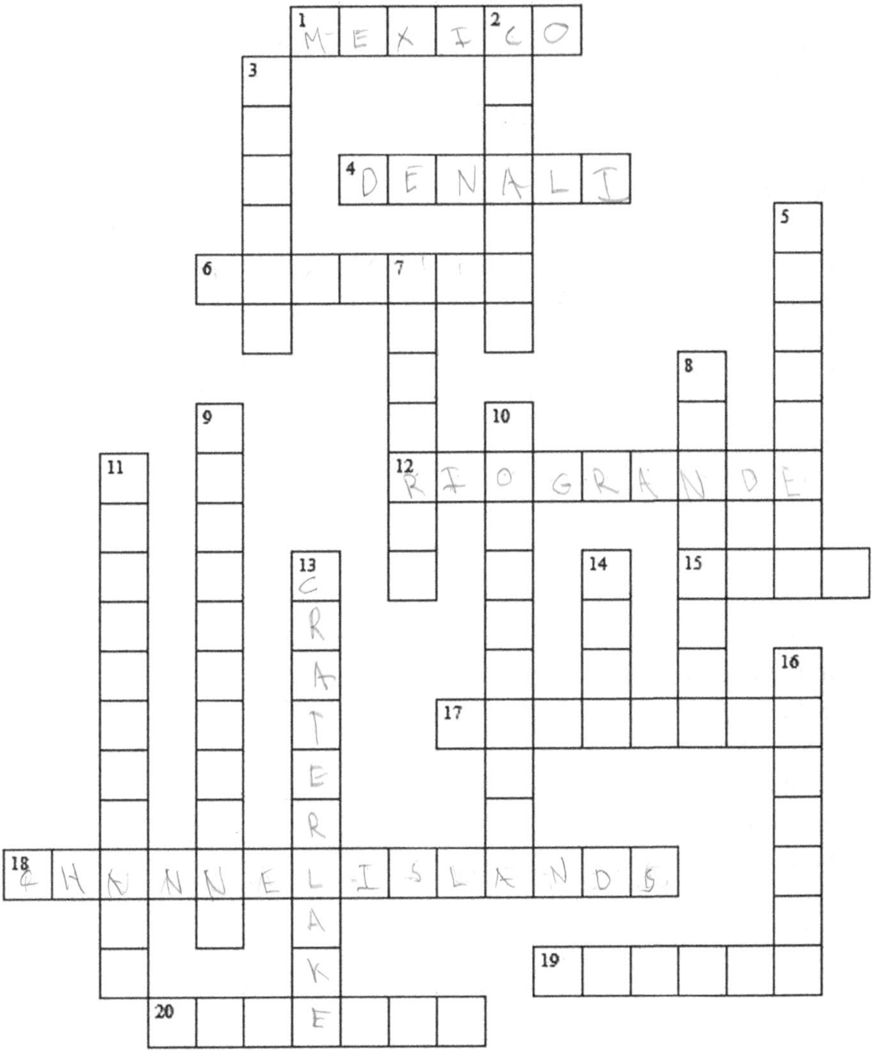

Caribbean Capitals

ACROSS

2. Haiti
4. Montserrat
5. Saint Vincent and the Grenadines
8. Barbados
10. Nicaragua
11. Dominica
14. Puerto Rico
15. Bahamas
16. Honduras
18. St. Kitts & Nevis
19. Bermuda
20. Trinidad & Tobago

DOWN

1. Belize
3. Cuba
6. Dominican Republic
7. Aruba
9. El Salvador
12. Costa Rica
13. Jamaica
17. St. Lucia

Caribbean Capitals

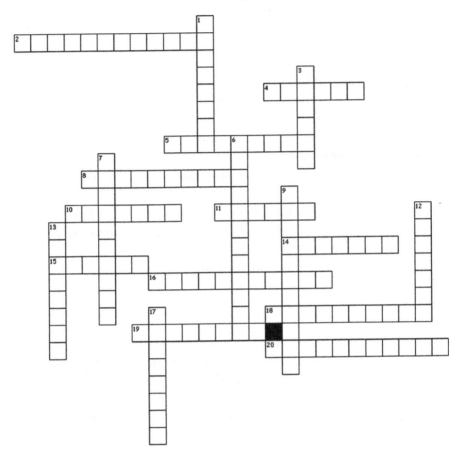

North and Central America, Part II

ACROSS

3. The second largest lake in Canada
8. The capital of Greenland, Godthab, is known by this other name
9. The Gaspe Peninsula is part of this Canadian province
10. The only Great Lake entirely within the U.S.
11. The largest state in Mexico
12. Fort-de-France is the capital of this French territory in the Lesser Antilles
13. Yukon Territory and British Columbia border this U.S. state
16. The Nicoya and Osa Peninsulas are in this Central American country with no army
19. The Dominican Republic and Haiti share this island

DOWN

1. This country in Central America borders only the Pacific Ocean
2. Lake Managua is located in this Central American country
4. The isthmus of _____ connects the main part of Mexico to the Yucatan Peninsula
5. Andros and Great Inagua are islands in this country in the Atlantic Ocean6. This passage separates Cuba and Hispaniola
7. Aruba and Curaçao belong to this country
14. This country is the easternmost of the Lesser Antilles
15. Cape Breton Island is part of this Canadian province
17. This island country near Venezuela is composed of two parts: Tobago and _____
18. This island is the 5th largest island in the world
19. Gonave Island belongs to this country

North and Central America - Part II

Chapter 3

South America

1. Quechua, a language spoken by which ancient civilization is still popular in South America?
    The Inca civilization

2. The world's highest navigable lake is situated to the north of the high plateau of Altiplano in Bolivia. Name this lake.
    Lake Titicaca

3. Llanos is a grassland region shared by Venezuela and which South American country bordering Panama?
    Colombia

4. Madidi National Park is in which landlocked country bordering Peru and Paraguay?
    Bolivia

5. The port of Callao serves the capital of Peru. Name this capital city.
    Lima

6. The ruins of Machu Picchu, situated near the historical city of Cusco, are an important attraction in which country north of Chile?
    Peru

7. The administrative capital of Bolivia is the world's highest national capital city. Name this city.
    La Paz

8. In 1498, which explorer became the first European to see the coast of South America?
    Christopher Columbus

9. Name the hot, wet region across the equatorial South America which contains the largest tropical rainforest in the world.
    Amazon basin

10. Name the most populous country in South America.
Brazil

11. Name the colder, desert landscape south of Pampas.
Patagonia

12. Name South America's largest island.
Tierra del Fuego

13. Lagoa dos Patos is considered to be one of the world's largest lagoons. This is situated in what country that has Sao Paulo as South America's largest metropolitan area?
Brazil

14. Rosario, on the Parana River, is a historic city in which large country whose southern region is dominated by the region of Patagonia?
Argentina

15. Pantanal, the world's largest freshwater wetland, is situated in which South American country where the majority of the population speaks Portuguese?
Brazil

16. Name the famous Andean mountain near Mendoza, Argentina.
Mount Aconcagua

17. Name the longest river in southern part of South America.
The Parana River

18. Name Argentina's largest metropolitan area.
Buenos Aires

19. Name the group of islands governed by the United Kingdom about 310 miles off the coast of Argentina that has Stanley as its capital city.
The Falkland Islands

20. Name the smaller of the two landlocked countries bordering Argentina.
Paraguay

21. Name the famous waterfalls on the Parana River on the Brazil-Argentina border.
Iguazu Falls

22. Name the French Overseas Department where the European Space Agency's spaceships could be launched from South America.
French Guiana

23. Georgetown is the capital which country bordering Brazil and Suriname?
Guyana

24. The Marajo Island lies near the delta of which major river in South America?
The Amazon

25. The world-famous Angel Falls is located in what country that has Caracas as its capital.
Venezuela

26. Name the only country in South America that has coastlines on both the Caribbean Sea and the Pacific Ocean.
Colombia

27. The Gran Chaco Region spans Argentina and what other country?
Paraguay

28. The Galapagos Islands on the Pacific belong to which country that has Guayaquil as its largest city?
Ecuador

29. The Valdes Peninsula is on what body of water?
The Atlantic Ocean

30. Easter Island, located in the Pacific Ocean, belongs to what country that has Antofagasta as an important coastal city?
Chile

31. Cuenca is a major city in the most densely populated country in South America. Name this country.
Ecuador

32. The cities of Asuncion and Concepcion are located on what river in the southern part of South America?
The Paraguay River

33. The Cotopaxi and the Chimborazo mountain peaks provide a magnificent view for tourists visiting what country whose major river is the Napo.
Ecuador

34. What is the dominant religion in South America?
Roman Catholicism

35. Name the second largest country in South America.
Argentina

36. Name the South American country that rejoined OPEC in 2007 after suspending its membership from December 1992 to October 2007.
Ecuador

37. Name the South American country that joined OPEC in 1960.
Venezuela

38. Marine Iguanas are native to what island group?
The Galapagos Islands

39. Name the South American country well-known for the mysterious Nazca lines found in its deserts.
Peru

40. Name the Brazilian city well-known for its carnival celebrations.
Rio de Janeiro

41. Which country is not landlocked—Uruguay, Paraguay, or Bolivia?
Uruguay

42. Brazil's most populous city was founded by Jesuit's mission in 1554. Name this coastal city.
Sao Paulo

43. Name the dry Chilean desert that straddles the Tropic of Capricorn.
The Atacama Desert

44. Valparaiso is a coastal city in which South American country bordering Argentina and Peru?
Chile

45. The Parana and the Uruguay rivers empty into the Rio de la Plata. The Rio de la Plata is an estuary that drains into what ocean?
The Atlantic Ocean

46. La Paz, Santa Cruz, Cochabamba are major cities in a landlocked South American country. Name this country.
Bolivia

47. Cartagena is a major South American city on the Caribbean. This is in what country?
Colombia

48. The Margarita Island and the La Tortuga Island belong to which oil-rich South American country?
Venezuela

49. Name the largest island in the Galápagos Islands.
Isabela

50. Name the high plateau that lies mostly in the western part of Bolivia.
Altiplano

51. The Chilean city of Antofagasta is situated on what desert?
The Atacama Desert

52. Name Uruguay's largest city.
Montevideo

53. Angel falls and Mount Roraima are located in Bolivar, the largest state in which South American country?
Venezuela

54. Which is closest to South America—Lesser Antilles or Greater Antilles?
Lesser Antilles

55. Gauchos are cattle herders found in Argentina and what small bordering country on the Atlantic Ocean?
Uruguay

56. Which is north—Guyana or Paraguay?
Guyana

57. Quito, South America's oldest capital, is in what country?
Ecuador

58. Name the islands administered by the United Kingdom off the Argentine coast in South America.
The Falkland Islands

59. Manaus, the largest city in the Amazon Basin, lies at the confluence of the Amazon River and what major tributary of the Amazon River?
The Negro River

60. Although Suriname consists of significant Asian population, what is its only official language?
Dutch

61. Trinidad and Tobago lie closest to which major river delta in South America?
The Orinoco River

62. In which country bordering Argentina would one find the Atacama Desert, some parts of which had their first rainfall after 400 years in 1971?
Chile

63. Name the world's longest mountain chain.
Andes

64. South American cowboys on the large ranches of Pampas are known by what name?
Gauchos

65. Name Uruguay's capital city on the Rio de la Plata.
Montevideo

66. Lake Maracaibo is an area that has rich deposits of oil in what South American country?
Venezuela

67. Cape Horn, the southernmost inhabited point in South America, belongs to what country?
Chile

68.   The Magdalena River is the lifeline of which South American
        country?
        Colombia

69.   Recife is an important city in what country?
        Brazil

70.   Tin is an important mineral export of which country—Bolivia or
        Uruguay?
        Bolivia

South America Rivers and Regions

ACROSS:

4. The former region of Gran Colombia comprised present-day Colombia, Venezuela, Panama, and _____
5. The mouth of the Amazon River is located at this major parallel
6. The Chonos Archipelago is off the coast of this country
7. The Brazilian city of Porto Alegre is situated on this lagoon
12. Second largest river in South America: _____ River
14. Rio de Janeiro enjoys stunning views of _____ Bay
16. This river is the largest river entirely within Brazil (2 words)
17. The _____ River forms the Amacura Delta in Venezuela
18. Swamp region in southwest Brazil

DOWN:

1. The Gulf of San Matias is north of this Argentine peninsula
2. The Salar de Uyuni salt pans are in the southwest of this landlocked country
3. The Altiplano is in these mountains
4. Colombia is the world's largest producer of this gem
7. Grasslands in central Argentina
8. The Colca Canyon is located just northwest of this Peruvian city
9. Asuncion is located on this river that cuts Paraguay in half: _____ River
10. The Guiana Highlands can be found in the Guianas, Brazil and this country
11. The _____ River forms the border between Peru and Colombia
13. Dry region in southern Argentina and part of Chile
15. The Maranon and this river combine to form the Amazon in Peru

South American Rivers and Regions

South America, Part II

ACROSS

2. This country was formerly known as Dutch Guiana
6. Buenos Aires shares the Rio de la Plata with this other capital
9. Cartagena, Colombia borders this ocean
11. The capital of France's small overseas department in South America
12. The largest city in Brazil
14. The Amazon originates in this country
15. The world's southernmost city, located in Argentina
16. Chile and Ecuador are the only two countries that don't border this country, the biggest in South America
17. Panama shares the Gulf of Darien with this country

DOWN

1. Giant tortoises are found in these islands belonging to Ecuador
3. The southern common market is also known as
4. The island that is located at the mouth of the Amazon River
5. The Bolivian Navy trains on this lake shared with Peru
7. This hydroelectric dam lies on the border of Paraguay and Brazil
8. Chimborazo is the highest point in this South American country on the equator
9. Tierra del Fuego, or "Land of Fire", is shared by Chile and _____
10. Angel Falls, the highest waterfall in South America, is in this country
13. This country has the second longest coastline in South America
14. Puerto Montt, located in Chile, is the southern end of the _____ Highway
16. This landlocked country has two capitals

<u>**South America** - Part II</u>

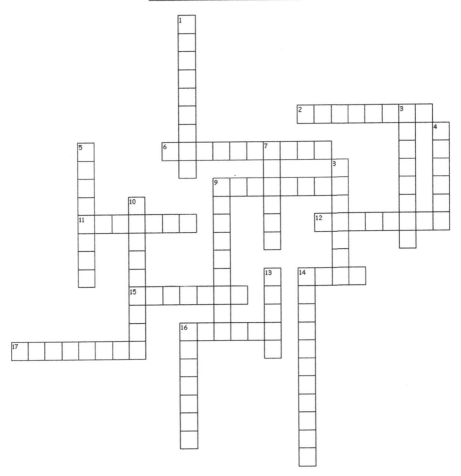

Chapter 4

Europe

1. The mouth of the Tagus River is in which body of water to the west of Portugal?
    The Atlantic Ocean

2. The historic city of Cordoba, located on the Guadalquivir River, is in what country bordering Andorra and France?
    Spain

3. The Balearic Islands, surrounded by the Balearic Sea, is part of what larger body of water?
    The Mediterranean Sea

4. The Bay of Biscay is shared by Spain and what other country?
    France

5. Name the small country situated on the French-Spanish border in the Pyrenees.
    Andorra

6. The Gulf of Lion is part of which sea?
    The Mediterranean Sea

7. The Rhone River, which rises in Switzerland, has its mouth in what country?
    France

8. The port cities of Calais and Dunkirk, in France, are situated on what strait?
    The Strait of Dover

9. Name the only country that borders Portugal.
    Spain

10. The city of Toulouse, on River Garonne, is located in what European country?
    France

11. Name France's largest city, located on River Seine.
    Paris

12. The cities of Tours and Orleans, on River Loire, are located in what country that borders Italy and Belgium?
    France

13. The Jura Mountains are shared by France and what other country?
    Switzerland

14. The St. Georges Channel separates Ireland from which principality of the United Kingdom?
    Wales

15. The capital city of Wales is located on the Bristol Channel. Name this city.
    Cardiff

16. Liverpool is England's major port on Mersey Estuary which is an extension of what sea?
    The Irish Sea

17. Name the island group, situated very close to France that is actually under the British Crown.
    The Channel Islands

18. Shannon and Limerick are major cities in which country north of the Celtic Sea?
    Ireland

19. Glasgow, on River Clyde, is the largest city in which political unit of the United Kingdom?
    Scotland

20. British Isles consists of two sovereign nations. Name these two nations.
    The United Kingdom and Ireland

21. Name the large Nordic country situated to the west of the Gulf of Bothnia.
Sweden

22. What name is commonly used to describe the historic regions of Norway, Sweden and Denmark?
Scandinavia

23. The Nordic countries mainly refer to Norway, Sweden, Denmark, and two other countries. Name these two countries.
Iceland and Finland

24. Hammerfest is considered by some to be mainland Europe's most northerly city. This is situated in which Scandinavian country to the west of Sweden?
Norway

25. The Jutland Peninsula belongs to which Nordic country?
Denmark

26. Name the largest island in the Kingdom of Denmark located between the Arctic Ocean and the North Atlantic Ocean.
Greenland

27. The Faeroe Islands, situated in the North Atlantic, belong to which country whose only mainland border is with Germany?
Denmark

28. Name the Nordic country that has a coast on the Kattegat and the Gulf of Bothnia and is the largest Nordic country by area.
Sweden

29. Name the Baltic state bordering Lithuania and Estonia whose capital city is near the mouth of the Daugava (Western Dvina) River.
Latvia

30. Rotterdam is the largest port in what country bordering Belgium and Germany?
Netherlands

31. Name the diamond-producing country that borders Luxembourg and Netherlands.
Belgium

32. The Ruhr Valley is one of the major industrial regions in which country that was divided after World War II and reunited after the end of the Cold War?
Germany

33. The Elbe River, which flows primarily in Germany, empties into what sea?
The North Sea

34. Vilnius is the capital of which country to the northwest of Belarus?
Lithuania

35. Lake Peipus is located on the border of Russia and which Baltic country on the Gulf of Finland?
Estonia

36. The towns of Vichy and Avignon are located in what country that borders Monaco?
France

37. Mont Blanc, the highest peak in Western Europe, is located in which country?
France

38. The Apennines form the backbone of what country that has coastlines along both the Adriatic Sea and the Tyrrhenian Sea?
Italy

39. Kosovo and what other landlocked country borders Montenegro?
Serbia

40. The city of Murmansk, on the Kola Peninsula, is located in what country bordering Estonia and Finland?
Russia

41. The Gulf of Messinia borders the southern shores of the Peloponnesus Peninsula of which European country?
Greece

42. The Bosporus Strait connects Turkey's Sea of Marmara to what body of water?
The Black Sea

43. Novi Sad, on River Danube, is an important city in which European country?
Serbia

44. The Balkan Peninsula takes its name from a mountain range of the same name in which country on the Black Sea bordered by the two landlocked countries of Macedonia and Serbia?
Bulgaria

45. Brasov is a mining town at the foothills of the Transylvanian Alps in what country?
Romania

46. France's closest point to the island of Great Britain is across what specific body of water?
Strait of Dover

47. The Prut River forms the border between Romania and which landlocked country to its east?
Moldova

48. Name the largest island in the Baltic Sea.
Gotland

49. Name Europe's westernmost country.
Iceland

50. Skopje is the capital of what landlocked European country?
Macedonia

51. Name Ukraine's largest river.
The Dnieper River

52. Constanta, Romania, is a major port on what body of water?
The Black Sea

53. The Pinsk Marshes is a wetland region found in northwest of Ukraine and which bordering country?
Belarus

54. Yalta, Ukraine is a port located on what peninsula?
Crimean Peninsula

55. Bratislava, capital of Slovakia, is on what major European river?
The Danube River

56. Wroclaw is an important manufacturing center in which country, the south of which shares the Carpathian Mountains with Slovakia?
Poland

57. Name the Russian exclave on the Baltic Sea that borders Poland and Lithuania.
Kaliningrad

58. One of the islands in the Comoros group in Africa is administered by France. Name this island.
Mayotte

59. Rome, Italy is located on what river?
The Tiber River

60. River Douro has its mouth near which Portuguese city?
Oporto

61. River Guadiana, which forms part of the border between Spain and Portugal, has its mouth in what gulf?
Gulf of Cadiz

62. Pico de Teide, Spain's highest peak, is on what island in the Canary Islands group?
Tenerife

63. The Vosges Mountains form France's border with which country?
Germany

64. The city of Paris is located near the confluence of the Marne and what river?
The Seine River

65. Ireland's highest peak is in what county that extends farthest west?
Kerry County

66. The Donegal Bay is located in which European country?
Ireland

67. Name the longest river in the United Kingdom.
The Severn River

68. Althing is the parliament of which European country?
Iceland

69. The French city of Strasbourg lies near the border of which country?
Germany

70. The island of Jan Mayen near Iceland belongs to what country?
Norway

71. The city of Visby, on the island of Gotland, belongs to what country?
Sweden

72. The historic coastal city of Ravenna lies in what country that owns the Elba Island?
Italy

73. Europoort, one of the largest human-made harbor and port complex is located in which European country?
Netherlands

74. What lake is shared by Germany, Switzerland and Austria?
Lake Constance

75. The Bay of Biscay lies to the north of what peninsula?
Iberian Peninsula

76. The Kerch Strait links the Sea of Azov to what sea?
The Black Sea

77. The Tyrrhenian Sea is situated to the west of which European country immersed in history?
Italy

78. What sea separates Africa from Europe?
The Mediterranean Sea

79. Name the European country that borders the Russian exclave of Kaliningrad to the south.
Poland

80. Dublin, Ireland is situated on the coast of what sea?
The Irish Sea

81. Name the European country, entirely within the continent, that extends farthest east.
Ukraine

82. The Strait of Gibraltar is the shortest route from the African mainland to what country in mainland Europe?
Spain

83. The country of Montenegro is on the coast of what body of water?
The Adriatic Sea

84. Most of the western shores of Scandinavia border what sea?
The Norwegian Sea

85. The Gulf of Bothnia separates Finland from which Scandinavian country?
Sweden

86. The Balearic Sea separates Balearic Islands from what European country to the west?
Spain

87. The Gulf of Finland is shared by Finland, Russia and what country bordering Latvia?
Estonia

88. Which lies farthest north—North Sea or the Norwegian Sea?
The Norwegian Sea

89. The series of wars fought between Christians and Muslim armies between 1096 and 1291 were known by what name?
Crusades

90. Corinth canal connects Gulf of Corinth and what body of water?
Saronic Gulf

91. Ljubljana is to Slovenia as Bern is to what?
Switzerland

92. Denmark's capital Copenhagen is located on what island?
Sjaelland

93. Lake Ohrid, the deepest lake in the Europe, is shared by Albania what other country?
Macedonia

94. The Inny, Suck, and Brosna are the tributaries of the longest river in Ireland. Name this river.
The Shannon River

95. Ulster and Munster are regions in a country that borders Celtic Sea to its southeast. Name this country.
Ireland

96. Oktoberfest, a major festival held in the fall in Munich since the 1800s, originated in what country?
Germany

97. Name the second largest city in Bosnia and Herzegovina on the Vrbas River.
Banja Luka

98. Name the second largest city and a major port of Albania.
Duress

99. The Thessaloniki film festival is held in which country?
Greece

100. Name the largest city in Wales.
Cardiff

101. Birmingham is a major city in the Midlands region of which European country?
United Kingdom

102. Horatio Nelson defeated the French at the Battle of Trafalgar off the coast of which present-day country?
Spain

103. Name the French city, well-known for its 1919 treaty signed by the Allies and Germany.
Versailles

104. On July 14, French citizens commemorate the storming of what French prison in 1789?
Bastille

105. Tiraspol, the capital of the self-proclaimed republic of Transnistria, is located in which landlocked country separated from Ukraine by the Dniester River?
Moldova

106. Swansea is the second largest city in which political unit of the United Kingdom?
Wales

107. What is the popular name for the Norse pirates from Scandinavia of the 9th and 10th centuries?
Vikings

108. In 1262, Iceland became a colony of which country that is a major producer of oil in Europe?
Norway

109. Granite from the quarries of Bornholm, south of Sweden, is an important resource for which country?
Denmark

110. Name Denmark's largest island outside of Greenland.
Sjaelland

111. Copenhagen, home to an automated, driverless metro system, is split between two islands in which country?
Denmark

112. The Oresund Bridge connects Copenhagen to which coastal city in Sweden?
Malmo

113. Mt. Vesuvius lies inland of what bay in Italy?
Bay of Naples

114. The Palio horse race in the Piazza del Campo is the biggest event in Siena, Italy. This city is in which Italian region?
Tuscany

115. Bremen, on the Weser River, is a major city in what European country?
Germany

116. Beethoven, a world-famous composer, was born in the capital city of former West Germany. Name this city.
Bonn

117. Name the isthmus that connects the Peloponnese Peninsula to mainland Greece.
Isthmus of Corinth

118. The Dodecanese Islands, which lies close to Turkey, belongs to what country?
Greece

119. Seville is a historic city in which country on the Iberian Peninsula?
Spain

120. What gulf lies to the north of Estonia?
Gulf of Finland

121. Podgorica is the capital of which Balkan country?
Montenegro

122. The Transylvanian Alps run through which country separated from Bulgaria by the Danube River?
Romania

123. Name the largest city in Croatia on the Sava River.
Zagreb

124. Ljubljana, the capital of Slovenia, is on what river?
The Sava River

125. The region of Dalmatia, in Croatia, is on what sea?
The Adriatic Sea

126. Name the highest peak in European Russia.
Mt. Elbrus

127. The Northern Dvina River in European Russia drains into what sea south of the Kola Peninsula?
The White Sea

128. The Crimean Peninsula belongs to which large country bordering Moldova and Belarus?
Ukraine

129. The Eiffel Tower is a famous structure in a European city known as the "City of Lights." Name this city.
Paris

130. Northern Ireland belongs to which European country—Ireland or the United Kingdom.
The United Kingdom

131.   What channel separates France from the United Kingdom?
The English Channel

132.   The Po River flows through the industrial region of what country?
Italy

133.   Stuttgart is a major city in which European country bordering Austria and Luxembourg?
Germany

134.   Nizhniy Novgorod is a major city in European Russia. This is located on Europe's longest river. Name this river.
The Volga River

135.   The Kanin Peninsula, bordered by the White Sea to the west, juts out into what sea that is to its north and east?
The Barents Sea

Europe, Part II

ACROSS

1. This strait separates Corsica and Sardinia
4. The Charles Bridge is in this capital
5. The only Baltic state that doesn't border Belarus
8. Hadrian's Wall is located near the border of England and _____
10. This river splits Budapest into the townships of Buda and Pest
11. Hamburg is at the mouth of the _____ River
12. Lyon is on this river
13. The easternmost European capital outside of Russia
16. Peninsula separated from Africa by the Strait of Gibraltar
18. Yalta is a port on this peninsula
19. This river separates Romania and Moldova
20. The Pindus Mountains are in the north of this country

DOWN

2. Oulu is a city in this country
3. Denmark occupies this peninsula
6. The Jura Mountains are on France's border with this country
7. Mallorca, Menorca, Ibiza and Formentera are in this island group
9. This island was home to the Minoan civilization
14. Cagliari and Bari are provinces in this country
15. This river passes through Rome
17. Istanbul is located on this strait

Europe - Part II

Chapter 5

Africa

1. Port Harcourt, a major port west of Cameroon, is located in what country?
    Nigeria

2. In Northwest Africa, Cape Verde is the least populous and the smallest country in area. This island country is in what body of water?
    The Atlantic Ocean

3. The Kano region, well-known for its peanut crop, is in the most populous country in Northwest Africa. Name this country on the Gulf of Guinea.
    Nigeria

4. The coastal city of Benghazi, Libya is situated on the Gulf of Sidra. This gulf is part of what major body of water?
    The Mediterranean Sea

5. Name the disputed Moroccan territory bordering Mauritania and Algeria.
    Western Sahara

6. The city of Bamako, Mali is on what important river that shares its name with an African country?
    The Niger River

7. The conflict-ridden region of Darfur is in what country south of Egypt?
    Sudan

8. What country with Mogadishu as its capital borders the Gulf of Aden?
    Somalia

9. Name the lake, world's third largest reservoir, formed by Egypt's Aswan High Dam.
    Lake Nasser

10. Name the smallest country in Northeast Africa that has the same name as its capital city.
Djibouti

11. Mount Kilimanjaro, Africa's highest peak, is in which East African country bordering Lake Tanganyika?
Tanzania

12. Name Tanzania's legislative capital.
Dodoma

13. Name the country on Lake Victoria that borders Kenya, Tanzania, and the Democratic Republic of the Congo.
Uganda

14. The Pyramids of Giza are found in what country?
Egypt

15. Name the disappearing African lake that shares its name with the country that has the Tibesti Mountains in its northern region.
Lake Chad

16. Name the Equatorial Central African country bordering Congo and Cameroon that has Libreville as its capital city.
Gabon

17. Name the channel that separates Madagascar from mainland Africa.
Mozambique Channel

18. The legislative capital of South Africa began as a Dutch supply station in 1652. Name this city.
Cape Town

19. The largest country in Southern Africa borders Namibia and the Democratic Republic of the Congo. Name this country.
Angola

20. Name Swaziland's legislative and royal capital.
Lobamba

21. An African country is famous for its high sand dunes and historically treacherous Skeleton Coast. Name this country that has Botswana to its east.
Namibia

22. Namibia's Caprivi Strip is bordered by Angola and which other landlocked country to its north that has Lusaka as its capital?
Zambia

23. The mouth of the Zambezi River is in what African country that shares its name with a channel on its eastern coast?
Mozambique

24. South Africa's administrative capital is sometimes known as Tshwane. What is its more commonly used name?
Pretoria

25. The Okavango Delta is situated in an African country that has Gaborone as its capital. Name this country.
Botswana

26. Name the landlocked African country that has the same name as a lake and borders Mozambique and Tanzania.
Malawi

27. The second cataract of the Nile River is situated in which country bordered by Eritrea and Ethiopia?
Sudan

28. The Danakil region in a Northeast African country is well-known for its findings of fossilized human remains from the prehistoric era. Name this country that shares Lake Turkana with Kenya.
Ethiopia

29. The small country of Djibouti is located on Bab-el-Mandeb that connects the Red Sea with what gulf?
Gulf of Aden

30. Ouagadougou is the capital of which small country bordering Ghana to its south?
Burkina Faso

31. Djenne is the oldest known city in Sub-Saharan Africa. This city is in what country that borders Cote D'Ivoire and Burkina Faso?
Mali

32. Name the East African capital city whose name in the Masai language translates to "Place of Cold Water."
Nairobi

33. Kisangani is an important city in which large country to the south of the Central African Republic.
Democratic Republic of the Congo

34. Name the only country that borders the northwest African country of Gambia.
Senegal

35. French is widely spoken in which country that is the source of River Niger and has Conakry as its major port city.
Guinea

36. Name the semi-desert scrubland on the southern edge of the Sahara stretching from Mauritania to Niger.
Sahel

37. If you are visiting the Great Zimbabwe ruins, you are closest to which capital city?
Harare

38. Mount Toubkal, in the High Atlas Mountains is the highest peak in the northern part of what country?
Morocco

39. The world's largest hot desert is found in Africa. Name this desert.
The Sahara Desert

40. Fort Mirabel, the training center for the French Foreign legion, is in which country bordering Tunisia and Libya?
Algeria

41. Name the major tributary of the Niger River.
The Benue River

42. Roumsiki is a beautiful village in the Mandara Mountains region of what country to the east of Nigeria?
Cameroon

43. The world's second deepest lake is also Africa's largest freshwater reservoir. Name this lake, which runs along the western boundary of Burundi.
Lake Tanganyika

44. Name the African river that supplies water to the stunning Victoria Falls, the widest cascade of water in the world, on the Zimbabwe-Zambian border.
The Zambezi River

45. The Chobe National Park is well-known for its herds of wild African elephants. This is in which landlocked country bordering Namibia and South Africa?
Botswana

46. When Romans conquered North Africa, they built the magnificent city of Volubilis in which country that is dominated by the

western section of the Atlas Mountains and located south of the Strait of Gibraltar?
Morocco

47. After the independence of South Sudan from former Sudan in July 2011, which Mediterranean country became Africa's largest country?
Algeria

48. Cabinda, on the Atlantic Ocean, is bordered by both the Republic of the Congo and the Democratic Republic of the Congo. This is an exclave of what country?
Angola

49. Name the well-known valley created by a fault that runs from the north to the south along Eastern Africa.
The Great Rift Valley

50. Rich deposits of diamonds and gold make which country the wealthiest in the southern Africa?
South Africa

51. The Aldabra Islands belong to a small archipelagic nation in the Indian Ocean. Name this country, which lies to the northeast of Comoros.
Seychelles

52. Name the landlocked country that borders only South Africa and Mozambique.
Swaziland

53. Bantu and San are indigenous people belonging to which part of Africa—Mediterranean Africa or sub-Saharan Africa?
Sub-Saharan Africa

54. The Niger River drains into what body of water in West Central Africa?
Gulf of Guinea

55. Nouakchott is the capital of an African country whose south-west border is formed entirely by the Senegal River. Name this country.
Mauritania

56. Bukavu shares a border with Rwanda. This is a town in which country that is Central Africa's largest and most populous?
Democratic Republic of the Congo

57. Name the second longest river in Africa.
The Congo River

58. In July 2009, President Barack Obama made a visit to a famous castle in the town of Cape Coast. This is in which country on the Gulf of Guinea that has English as its official language?
Ghana

59. Cape Agulhas is the southernmost point in mainland Africa. This is in what country?
South Africa

60. The Tropic of Capricorn passes through which large African island country?
Madagascar

61. Brazzaville is to the Republic of the Congo as Kinshasa is to what?
Democratic Republic of the Congo

62. Bangui is the capital of an African country to the east of Cameroon. Name this country.
Central African Republic

63. Victoria is the capital of which African island country in the Indian Ocean?
Seychelles

64. French is the official language of which African island country that has Port Louis as its capital?
Mauritius

65. If you are visiting a famous souk or market in Fez, you are in which African country that is northwest of Algeria and borders the Mediterranean Sea?
Morocco

66. The mouth of the Nile River is in which region—Lower Egypt or Upper Egypt?
Lower Egypt

67. During the fifteenth century, the kingdom of Benin flourished in West Africa in what present-day country, the largest country on the Niger Delta?
Nigeria

68. Libreville, Lambarene, and Franceville are cities of a country that straddles the equator. Name this country.
Gabon

69. The capital and largest city of Gambia lies at the mouth of the Gambia River. Name this city.
Banjul

70. Name the most populous Atlantic coast city in South Africa.
Cape Town

71. Name the small country that Somalia borders to its northwest.
Djibouti

72. Which port city in Somalia is just south of Equator—Kisimayo or Mogadishu?
Kisimayo

73. Which country in southeastern Africa was once a Portuguese colony?
Mozambique

74. Which country is the largest of the present-day kingdoms in Africa—Morocco or Lesotho?
Morocco

75. Timbuktu, a UNESCO World Heritage Site, is in which country?
Mali

76. The Senegal River forms border between Senegal and what other country to its north?
Mauritania

77. Cape Town is located at the northern end of the Cape Peninsula. Cape Peninsula juts into what Ocean?
The Atlantic Ocean

78. The Hassan II Mosque, the third largest mosque in the world, is located in the largest port city in North Africa. Name this city.
Casablanca

79. In 1973, Libya claimed what gulf to be within Libyan territorial waters?
Gulf of Sidra

80. What is the largest city in Sub-Saharan Africa?
Lagos, Nigeria

81. Name the largest monolith statue in the world on the west bank of Nile near Cairo, Egypt.
The Great Sphinx of Giza

82. Name the landlocked country in Central Africa that borders Sudan, Chad and Cameroon.
Central African Republic

83. Name Africa's second highest mountain.
   Mount Kenya

84. Siam is to Thailand as Zaire is to what?
   Democratic Republic of the Congo

85. Name Kenya's largest port.
   Mombasa

86. Lubumbashi is the most populated city in the southern part of which country that borders South Sudan and Zambia?
   Democratic Republic of the Congo

87. Port Elizabeth is an important port in which African country bordering Botswana and Mozambique?
   South Africa

88. Burkina Faso was known by what name when the French ruled the land until 1960?
   Upper Volta

89. Name the ethnic group of mostly mixed black African and Indonesian ancestry in Madagascar.
   Malagasy

90. Name Zambia's most important commodity.
   Copper

91. Name the nomadic group that lived in the Sinai for several centuries.
   Bedouins

92. Sousse, located north of Sfax on the Gulf of Hammamet, is a major city in Mediterranean Africa's smallest country by area. Name this country.
   Tunisia

93. In 1989, Libya signed a peace agreement with which country that resulted in its withdrawal from the Tibesti Mountain region?
Chad

94. 622 A.D. marks the beginning of the Islamic year when Prophet Mohammad departed from Mecca to which holy city?
Medina

95. Ghiblis in Libya describe what physical phenomenon – Sandstorm or Wind?
Wind

96. What major Egyptian engineering feat was inspired by Frenchman Ferdinand de Lesseps?
The Suez Canal

97. The Qattara Depression is the largest in which African country bordering the Mediterranean and Red Seas?
Egypt

98. In 1867, diamonds were discovered in Kimberley in the Northern Cape Province of which African country?
South Africa

99. Lake Turkana is shared by Kenya and what other country that borders Eritrea and Kenya?
Ethiopia

100. Name Tanzania's administrative capital.
Dar es Salaam

101. Lamu Island, in the Indian Ocean, belongs to what equatorial country?
Kenya

102. The island of Bioko, in the Gulf of Guinea, belongs to what country?
Equatorial Guinea

103. Mahajanga, on the Mozambique Channel, is an important city in what country that straddles the Tropic of Capricorn?
Madagascar

104. Blantyre is a major city in what country that has Lilongwe as its capital?
Malawi

105. Lake Kariba borders Zambia and what country bordering Botswana?
Zimbabwe

106. Virunga mountains are located at the junction of Rwanda, Democratic Republic of the Congo and what other country?
Uganda

107. El Fasher is a major city in which country bordering Ethiopia and Libya?
Sudan

108. Feluccas are sailboats that carry goods and people along the Nile River. The Nile River's mouth is in which country—Egypt or Sudan?
Egypt

109. Ibn Batuta, the world famous traveler, was born in Tangier in what country that lies just south of the Strait of Gibraltar?
Morocco

110. Lake Tana is considered by many as the source of the Nile River. This is in what country?
Ethiopia

African Cities

ACROSS:

1. Kenya's main port
5. This Liberian city was settled by freed slaves
6. The Malinese city where a mud mosque is reconstructed each year
8. Located on the island of Bioko, the capital of the only Spanish-speaking country in Africa
10. Second largest city in Botswana
12. The former capital of Nigeria
15. Primary copper-mining city of Zambia
16. Named after a current, this city is the second largest port in Angola
17. This capital city, near the Great Zimbabwe ruins, was formerly known as Salisbury
18. The second largest city in the Maghreb, it is home to the Casbah
19. Cote d'Ivoire main port

DOWN:

2. Egyptian city home to a famous lighthouse
3. Gold mines in South Africa are centered at this major city, also known for the Soweto choir
4. This Nigerian city is the ancient Hausa capital
6. Westernmost capital on the mainland of Africa
7. This Zambian city is located on Victoria Falls
9. Headquarters of the African Union
11. Located in Namibia, this city was once occupied by South Africa
13. The legislative capital of South Africa
14. The capital city that borders Brazzaville across the Congo River

African Cities

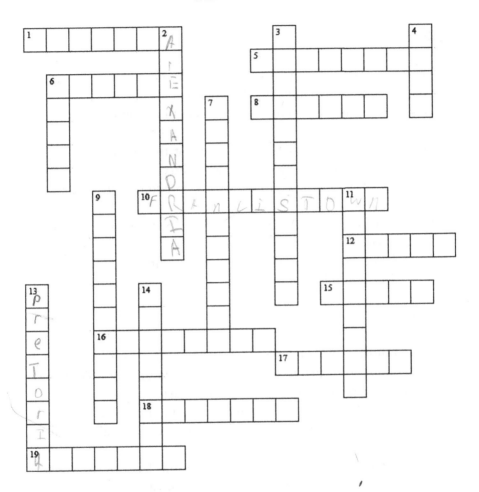

2. A L E X A N D R I A

10. F R A N K I S T O W N

13. P r e I O r I A

Africa, Part II

ACROSS

3. The country that uses the naira as their currency
6. The Gambia is surrounded by this country
8. Ceuta and Melilla are Spanish territories in this country
10. The currency of Angola
11. The Ahaggar Mountains are in the south of this country
12. The source of the Blue Nile is in this country
14. The Dogon are an ethnic group that lives predominantly in this country
15. This French dependency was once part of the Comoros Islands
16. Pemba Island belongs to this country
18. The delta of the Limpopo River is in this country
19. Walvis Bay is in this country

DOWN

1. Westernmost capital of Africa
2. This country is located to the west of the Central African Republic
4. This country is also known as the Gold Coast
5. The Senegal River passes through Senegal and this other country
7. The intersection of the Equator and the Prime Meridian is in this gulf
8. Mozambique, Malawi and Tanzania border this lake
9. The country was once called Southern Rhodesia
13. The Gulf of Hamamet is found in this country
17. The capital of Equatorial Guinea is located on this island

Africa - Part II

Chapter 6

Asia

1. What is eastern Asia's staple grain crop?
   Rice

2. The Trans-Siberian Railway runs from Moscow to which city on the Pacific coast?
   Vladivostok

3. The Chukchis are the dominant native people in which region of Asian Russia?
   Siberia

4. What gulf lies to the east of the Yamal Peninsula?
   Gulf of Ob

5. The Amur River forms part of the border between China and which large country to its north?
   Russia

6. What mountains define part of the border between Asian Russia and European Russia?
   Ural Mountains

7. Name the sea north of the Sakhalin Islands and southwest of the Kamchatka Peninsula.
   The Sea of Okhotsk

8. The Kuril Islands lie between Russia's Kamchatka Peninsula and which other country?
   Japan

9. The Bering Sea is part of what ocean?
   The Pacific Ocean

10. Russia's Laptev and Kara seas are part of what ocean?
    The Arctic Ocean

11. Lake Balkhash is in Central Asia's largest country. Name this country.
Kazakhstan

12. Qizilqum Desert dominates Central Asia's most populous country. Name this country.
Uzbekistan

13. Ulaanbaatar is the capital of Central Asia's least populous country. Name this country that shares the Gobi Desert with China.
Mongolia

14. The Pamir Mountains dominate which Central Asian country that has Dushanbe as its capital?
Tajikistan

15. The Garagum Desert occupies most of which country that is bordered by Kazakhstan, Iran, and the Caspian Sea?
Turkmenistan

16. The Tian Shan Mountains separate China from what country that has Bishkek as its capital?
Kyrgyzstan

17. Incheon is a historic city in East Asia's smallest country east of the Yellow Sea. Name this country.
South Korea

18. The Yalu and the Tumen Rivers form China's border with East Asia's least populous country. Name this country.
North Korea

19. The Three Gorges Dam in China is built across Asia's longest river. Name this river.
The Yangtze River (Chang River)

20. Name the large island to the east of China that straddles the Tropic of Cancer.
Taiwan

21. Hong Kong is located on what sea?
The South China Sea

22. Name China's largest city on the coast of the East China Sea.
Shanghai

23. Inner Mongolia is situated in what East Asian country?
China

24. China's Tarim River flows along the northern part of what large desert in the Sinkiang region?
The Taklimakan Desert

25. The Seikan Tunnel connects the island of Hokkaido with Honshu. This is in what country that has Osaka as a major city?
Japan

26. Tyre and Sidon are important coastal cities in what Eastern Mediterranean country bordering Syria and Israel?
Lebanon

27. The Sea of Galilee is located in which country to the east of Egypt?
Israel

28. Petra is an important tourist site in what country bordering Saudi Arabia, Iraq, and Israel?
Jordan

29. What famous river exits Syria on its Iraqi border?
The Euphrates

30. Yerevan is the capital of which country bordering Azerbaijan, Georgia, and Turkey?
Armenia

31. Georgia and Turkey share what sea along with several other countries in the region?
The Black Sea

32. The Dardanelles Strait connects the Sea of Marmara with what arm of the Mediterranean Sea?
The Aegean Sea

33. What strait connects the Sea of Marmara with the Black Sea?
The Bosphorus Strait

34. Farsi is the most widely spoken language in what country that has Mt. Damavand as its highest peak?
Iran

35. The Zagros Mountains are the most dominant range in what country to Pakistan's west?
Iran

36. Name the strait that separates the exclave of Oman on the Musandam Peninsula from Iran.
The Strait of Hormuz

37. Majority of the residents of Nagorno-Karabakh, an Armenian enclave in Azerbaijan, follow what religion?
Christianity

38. The world's largest sand desert, Rub' al-Khali or the "Empty Quarter," is located in the largest country on the Arabian Peninsula. Name this country.
Saudi Arabia

39. Sharjah is one of the seven emirates in which country on the Arabian Peninsula?
The United Arab Emirates

40. The Islamic holy cities of Mecca and Medina are located in which country bordered by Oman and Iraq?
Saudi Arabia

41. The smallest country in South Asia in both population and area is located to the south of the island of Minicoy. Name this country in the Indian Ocean.
Maldives

42. Name the mountainous Buddhist kingdom bordering India and China.
Bhutan

43. Name the present-day island country that was formerly known as Ceylon.
Sri Lanka

44. The mouths of the Ganges River are located in which densely populated South Asian country?
Bangladesh

45. Name India's highest peak.
Mount Kanchenjunga

46. The Deccan Plateau lies between the Eastern and Western Ghats in what country?
India

47. The Great Indian Desert extends westwards to which country that has most of the Indus River?
Pakistan

48. Helmand River is a major river in what country bordering Pakistan and Uzbekistan?
Afghanistan

49. Chittagong is a major port in what country bordering Myanmar along the coast of the Bay of Bengal?
Bangladesh

50. Bagan and Mandalay are important cities in what South Asian country whose administrative capital is Nay Pyi Taw?
Myanmar (Burma)

51. The Chao Phraya is a major river in the largest country in Southeast Asia. Name this country.
Thailand

52. The smallest country in Southeast Asia is an island off the southern tip of the Malay Peninsula. Name this country.
Singapore

53. Bandar Seri Begawan is the capital of a country with the highest GDP in Southeast Asia bordering the South China Sea. Name this country.
Brunei

54. Name highly populous country in Southeast Asia that consists of the islands of Mindanao and Luzon.
The Philippines

55. George Town is an important city in which Southeast Asian country whose peninsular territory is separated from Indonesia by the Strait of Malacca?
Malaysia

56. Tonle Sap, Southeast Asia's largest freshwater lake, is located in which country south of Thailand?
Cambodia

57. The mouth of the Mekong River is in what country on the South China Sea?
Vietnam

58. Lounagphrabang, a major city in Laos, is on what river?
The Mekong River

59. Name the only country in Southeast Asia that was never under a colonial power.
Thailand

60. Name the world's largest island nation.
Indonesia

61. Name the smallest predominantly Catholic country in Asia.
East Timor

62. Name the country that has the world's largest Muslim population.
Indonesia

63. Borneo is separated from the island of Celebes by what strait?
Makassar Strait

64. The Indonesian territory on the island of New Guinea is separated from Australia by what sea?
The Arafura Sea

65. Bandung is a major city in Indonesia's most populous island. Name this island.
Java

66. The city of Banda Aceh on the northwestern tip of Sumatra, Indonesia, is on the coast of what sea?
The Andaman Sea

67. Name the gulf between Vietnam and the island of Hainan.
Gulf of Tonkin

68. Name Myanmar's legislative capital to the east of the Irrawaddy River Delta.
    Yangon

69. The holy city of Varanasi, India, is on what river?
    The Ganges River

70. Name the highest peak in the Karakoram Range in Asia.
    K2 (Godwin Austen)

71. The ruins of Persepolis are an important historic site in what country that has Dasht-e Kavir (Salt Desert) and the Dasht-e Lut as its major desert regions?
    Iran

72. Manama is the capital of what small country connected to Saudi Arabia by the King Fahd Causeway?
    Bahrain

73. Name the largest city on the Tigris River in the historical Mesopotamian region.
    Baghdad

74. The northwestern corner of Saudi Arabia is separated from Egypt by what gulf?
    Gulf of Aqaba

75. Name the most populous country in Southwest Asia that has Lake Urmia as its largest lake.
    Iran

76. Majority of the people in Nepal follow what religion?
    Hinduism

77. Erzurum is a major city near the source of the Euphrates River in the largest country in the Eastern Mediterranean region of Asia. Name this country.
    Turkey

78. Punjab is a region both in India and in which other country?
Pakistan

79. The Lena River is one of the major rivers in what country bordering Finland and Estonia?
Russia

80. The Baikonur Cosmodrome is managed by the Russian Federal Agency. This space flight launch center is located in what country that has Astana as its capital?
Kazakhstan

81. The important port of Basra is at the end of the Shatt-al Arab. This is in which Southwest Asian country with a Shia Muslim majority?
Iraq

82. Nagasaki is a city in Japan's southernmost major island. Name this island.
Kyushu

83. Mount Fuji is on Japan's largest island. Name this island.
Honshu

84. The largest island in Thailand is located in the Andaman Sea. Name this island.
Phuket

85. Most of the population follows Theravada Buddhism in a country directly west of Thailand. Name this country.
Myanmar

86. Name the landlocked country in Asia where the majority of the population follows Hinduism.
Nepal

87. Mecca is to Saudi Arabia as Karbala is to what?
Iraq

88. What body of water borders both Saudi Arabia and Iran?
The Persian Gulf

89. Which small neighboring country was invaded by Iraq in 1990-91?
Kuwait

90. The heart of Ottoman Empire was in which eastern Mediterranean country?
Turkey

91. What large lake borders Iran to the north?
The Caspian Sea

92. Iraq has a short border with what country that has Aqaba as its major port city?
Jordan

93. Doha is to Qatar as Sana'a is to what?
Yemen

94. What major line of latitude runs through Taiwan?
The Tropic of Cancer

95. Beirut and Tel Aviv are major port cities on what sea?
The Mediterranean Sea

96. Da Nang, Hue, Vinh, and Nha Trang are important cities on the South China Sea of which country?
Vietnam

97. What is the financial capital of Israel?
Tel Aviv

98. Akshardham Temple, on the banks of River Yamuna, is the world's biggest Hindu Temple and receives 100,000 visitors a week. This temple is located in what South Asian country?
India

99. Which is north—Tashkent or Astana?
Astana

100. The mouth of the Salween River is in what country that is east of India?
Myanmar (Burma)

101. Pahang is the largest state of a country where Ringgit is the official currency. Name this country.
Malaysia

102. The Deccan Plateau is to India as the Korat Plateau is to what?
Thailand

103. The Sunda Strait separates Java and what large island in Indonesia?
Sumatra

104. Name the longest river in Asia.
The Yangtze River

105. Formosa, meaning "beautiful island", is the largest island of the Republic of China. What is the present day name of this island?
Taiwan

106. The Yucatan Peninsula is to Mexico as the Yamal Peninsula is to what?
Russia

107. Ha Long Bay lies off the northern coast of what country once colonized by France?
Vietnam

108. Negev desert forms most of the southern part of what country?
Israel

109. If you are in Hanoi celebrating Tet, the New Year festival, you are in which country?
Vietnam

110. Indonesia and what other country border Malaysia on the island of Borneo?
Brunei

111. Gulf of Tonkin is part of what sea?
The South China Sea

112. The Sea of Galilee is located in northeastern part of which country?
Israel

113. Madras is to Chennai as Saigon is to what?
Ho Chi Minh City

114. Jeddah and Riyadh are located in what Middle Eastern country—Saudi Arabia or Iraq?
Saudi Arabia

115. Manchuria, a region south of the Amur River, is in what Asian country?
China

116. Ulaanbaatar is the largest city in what country?
Mongolia

117. Mashhad is a major city in which country bordering Pakistan and Turkey?
Iran

118. Name the country that does not border Afghanistan—
Turkmenistan, Uzbekistan, or Kazakhstan.
Kazakhstan

119. Perm, a major city west of the Ural Mountains, is in what
country?
Russia

120. Yakutsk, a major city on the Lena River, is in what country?
Russia

121. Jaipur, nicknamed the "pink city", is in the largest country in
mainland Asia south of the Himalayas. Name this country.
India

122. The Kaliningrad region on the coast of the Baltic Sea is an
exclave of the largest country in the world. Name this country.
Russia

123. Konya is an important city in the largest country in the Eastern
Mediterranean region. Name this country.
Turkey

124. Baku, Azerbaijan's capital city, lies on the shores of the world's
largest lake. Name this lake.
Caspian Sea

125. Yellow Sea is to China as Laptev Sea is to what?
Russia

126. The Mount Everest, world's highest peak, is in what country—
Nepal or India?
Nepal

127. The Arctic Circle passes through what country—Russia or China?
Russia

128. Japan's fertile Niigata Plains are drained by the country's longest river. Name this river.
Shinano River

129. Rupiah is to Indonesia as Ngultrum is to what?
Bhutan

130. Name the Southeast Asian country whose two major sections are spread over Borneo and the Malay Peninsula.
Malaysia

Asia Landforms

ACROSS

2. This large plateau covers much of central India: _____ Plateau
4. Varanasi, Allahabad and Kanpur are on this sacred Indian River: _____ River
8. Major rivers like the Ganges, the Brahmaputra, the Indus, and the Yangtze rise in these mountains
9. The largest country on this peninsula is Saudi Arabia: _____ Peninsula
10. The cold desert shared by Mongolia and China: _____ Desert
15. These mountains, along with the Ural River, form the western boundary of Asia: _____ Mountains
18. The longest river of Pakistan
19. Most Indian rivers (except the Narmada and Tapti) flow ultimately into this body of water
20. his Chinese region was occupied by the Japanese during WWII

DOWN

1. The mouth of Shatt al-Arab is in this gulf
3. The other name for Great Indian Desert
5. Russian prisoners were sent to this cold, harsh region
6. 3rd longest river in the world: _____ River
7. The large, crescent-shaped lake in Kazakhstan
11. Located in eastern Russia, Lake _____ is the deepest in the world.
12. This sea on the eastern coast of Korean Peninsula
13. The Ob and Irtysh rivers have their source in these mountains
14. Loess deposits, carried by wind, are found all along this river in Northern China
16. 3rd largest ocean in the world: _____ Ocean
17. Mountain system that forms the northern border of Tibetan Plateau

Asian Landforms

Asia, Part II

ACROSS

6. The rapidly dissolving Aral Sea lies between Kazakhstan and
_____

8. Aleppo is a city in this country
10. The capital of Kazakhstan until 1997
11. The currency of Bhutan
12. The United Arab Emirates cuts off the Musandam Peninsula from the main part of this country
13. The Inland Sea is in this country
14. The Harirud River has its source in this country
17. Ceylon is the former name for this country
19. This river is most voluminous that originates from the Himalayas

DOWN

1. The Cardamom Mountains are in this country
2. Konya and Antalya are cities in this country
3. The capital of Hong Kong
4. China borders Afghanistan through the _____ Corridor
5. The Rann of Kutch is in Gujarat in this country
7. The Sibuyan Sea borders Panay and Mindoro in this country
9. The southernmost country on the Arabian Peninsula
14. Irian Jaya is bordered by this sea to the south
15. The Ha Long Bay separates Vietnam from this island to the east
16. This city is Israel's principal port on the Gulf of Aqaba
18. The Tian Shan Mountains are shared by China and this country

Asia, Part II

Chapter 7

Australia, Oceania, and Antarctica

1. Name the highest point in the region that comprises Australia,
    New Zealand, and Oceania.
    Mt. Wilhelm

2. The Eucla Basin, south of the Great Victoria Desert, lies on the
    coast of what body of water?
    The Great Australian Bight

3. Mt. Cook, New Zealand's highest peak, is on what island?
    South Island

4. The island nation of Vanuatu is located in what body of water?
    The Pacific Ocean

5. What gulf is situated to the west of Australia's Cape York
    Peninsula?
    Gulf of Carpentaria

6. A majority of the Pacific island countries are located to the north
    of what major line of latitude?
    The Tropic of Capricorn

7. Name the longest river system in Australia.
    The Murray-Darling River System

8. The Great Artesian Basin and Mt. Kosciuszko are located in what
    large country in the Southern Hemisphere?
    Australia

9. Name Australia's largest island state.
    Tasmania

10. What strait separates Tasmania from mainland Australia?
    The Bass Strait

11. Australia's Great Barrier Reef is in what sea?
    The Coral Sea

12. The Australian city of Perth is on what body of water?
The Indian Ocean

13. Which country is closer to Australia —Papua New Guinea or New Zealand?
Papua New Guinea

14. The Cook Strait separates which two major islands in New Zealand?
North Island and South Island

15. The city of Christchurch is on the largest island in New Zealand. Name this island.
South Island

16. Mt. Taranaki or Mt. Egmont, located in the southwestern part of New Zealand's North Island, is on what sea?
The Tasman Sea

17. Milford Sound is a major tourist destination on what island in New Zealand that is well-known for its beautiful sceneries and stunning glaciers?
South Island

18. Mt. Cook is the highest point in what mountains that dominate the western part of New Zealand's South Island?
The Southern Alps

19. Dunedin and Invercargill are located on what island north of the Foveaux Strait?
South Island

20. Tahiti belongs to which European country?
France

21. Melanesia extends from Fiji to which country that has Port Moresby as its capital?
Papua New Guinea

22. The island nation of Palau is in what region —Micronesia or Melanesia?
Micronesia

23. Tahiti and Samoa belong to what region—Micronesia or Polynesia?
Polynesia

24. The Arafura Sea separates Australia from what large island?
New Guinea

25. Majuro is the capital of what Pacific country?
Marshall Islands

26. Melekeok is the capital of which country located near the western extent of the Caroline Islands?
Palau

27. The Drake Passage separates South America from which continent?
Antarctica

28. The MacDonnell Range is located in the central region of which country?
Australia

29. Name the maze of coral reefs stretching 1200 miles along the northeastern coast of Australia.
The Great Barrier Reef

30. Many consider the dingo-proof fence around Queensland's main sheep-grazing areas as the world's longest fence. This is located in what country?
Australia

31. Geysers in the region of Rotorua are used to drive electric power stations in which country that gained independence from Britain in 1907?
New Zealand

32. The dark-skinned Melanesians in the Pacific region are closely related to the native Aborigines in what country?
Australia

33. Name the descendants of the Polynesians who settled in New Zealand in 900 A.D.
Maoris

34. Vinson Massif, on the Ellsworth Mountains, is the highest peak on what continent?
Antarctica

35. McMurdo Sound is an extension of what sea in Antarctica?
The Ross Sea

36. The Antarctic Peninsula is closest to what continent?
South America

37. Polar bears are not found in which of these places—the Arctic, Antarctica, or Canada?
Antarctica

38. The Uluru Peak, a massive rock structure, rises in the middle of which continent?
Australia

39. The Bellingshausen Sea and the Ross Sea are extensions of what ocean?
The Pacific Ocean

40. The Weddell Sea in Antarctica is an extension of what ocean?
The Atlantic Ocean

41. Name the mountain range that separates East Antarctica from West Antarctica.
Trans-Antarctic Mountains

42. One of the world's richest ecosystems is situated in an area where the southern regions of the world's oceans meet the cold Antarctic Circumpolar Current. Name this region.
Antarctic Convergence or Antarctic Polar Front

43. South Shetland Islands lie closer to which Antarctic region?
Antarctic Peninsula

44. Mount Erebus, the world's southernmost volcano, is in what continent?
Antarctica

45. The Sydney Opera House is located in what country?
Australia

46. Dampier Land is located on the Indian Ocean coast of what country?
Australia

47. Palmyra Atoll and Jarvis Island, part of the Line Islands, a group that extends from the North Pacific to the South Pacific. These two islands belong to what country?
United States

48. Pitcairn Island and the Henderson Island, in the South Pacific, belong to what country?
United Kingdom

49. The Volcano Islands and the Bonin Islands, belong to what country?
Japan

50. The Amundsen-Scott Station, the United States' station near the geographic South Pole, is located on what plateau?
Polar Plateau

Australia, Oceania and Antarctica

ACROSS:

4. Australia's third largest city.
6. This city on the Swan River is the capital of West Australia.
7. _____ Island is separated from South Island of New Zealand by the Foveaux Strait.
13. Oceania's highest peak is in this country
14. The other name for Ayers Rock.
16. The _____ Ice Shelf is the second largest in Antarctica.
18. Australia and this continent lie entirely in the Southern Hemisphere.
19. This peak, the highest in Antarctica, is in the Sentinel Range.
20. This country has the Pa'anga as its currency.

DOWN:

1. The _____ Mountains separate East and West Antarctica.
2. The _____ Bay is also known as the Bay of Plenty.
3. Auckland is located on ___ ____of New Zealand
5. This national park, located in Australia's Northern Territory, is filled with Aboriginal Culture.
8. This Australian state is named for Dutch explorer Abel Tasman.
9. Both a type of bird and a citizen of New Zealand are named this.
10. The most densely populated state in Australia.
11. This country, with a capital of Funafuti, has a name that means "Group of Eight."
12. The ___ Sea is located to the northeast of Australia.
15. Melbourne is on the _____ River.
17. This city, the capital of Tasmania, is on the Derwent River.

Australia, Antarctica & Oceania

Australia, Oceania and Antarctica, Part II

ACROSS

1. The highest point in Papua New Guinea is Mount _____
4. This island is located in Antarctica's largest ice shelf
5. Wellington is on this island of New Zealand
7. This is the second largest island in the world
12. The capital of Samoa
14. The Gulf of _____ is west of the Cape York Peninsula in Australia
18. The Bay of Plenty is also known as _____ Bay
19. This country is known as the Gilbert Islands while under British occupation
20. This sea is north of the Antarctic Peninsula

DOWN

2. The Solomon Islands are part of this larger group of islands in the South Pacific
3. The strait that separates South Island and Steward Island
6. Norfolk Island belongs to this country
8. This country has a research station at the South Pole
9. The Great Barrier Reef lies off of this Australian province
10. The present-day name for the Sandwich Islands
11. The Cook Islands belong to this country
13. Challenger Deep, the lowest point in the world, is in the waters belonging to the _____ Islands
15. Currency of Vanuatu
16. Lesser Antarctica borders this ocean
17. The capital of French Polynesia is located on this island

Australia, Oceania and Antarctica - Part II

Chapter 8

Physical Geography

1. Fetch is the distance traveled by waves without interruption. Does a longer fetch result in bigger waves or smaller waves?
Bigger waves

2. What is the term for the lowest tides of the month—Neap Tides or Spring Tides?
Neap Tides

3. A wind that blows mainly from one direction could result in the formation of ocean currents. What is the term for these winds— Prevailing Winds or Hurricane Winds?
Prevailing Winds

4. What term describes a scientist who studies the origin, structure, and physical nature of the earth—Geologist or Paleontologist?
Geologist

5. A steep incline separates the ocean bed from the shallower seabed near a continent. This incline is known by what term— Continental Slope or Continental Divide?
Continental Slope

6. A small piece of high land that juts out into the sea is a headland. A much larger piece of land that has the same shape is known by what term—Cliff or Peninsula?
Peninsula

7. What term describes a narrow channel that links one body of water to another—Strait or Isthmus?
Strait

8. What is the term for a tall, vertical rock formation in the sea, separated from the cliffs of the headland region from which it was eroded—Sandbar or a Stack?
Stack

9. What common term describes a large sand bank piled up by the wind—a Sand Dune or a Sand Hill?
Sand Dune

10. A deep depression in the ocean bed is known by what term— Trench or Sinkhole?
Trench

11. What is the most basic material in most cave formations— Fossilite or Calcite?
Calcite

12. What term describes a large, thick mass of ice and snow that moves very slowly down a slope—River or Glacier?
Glacier

13. What term describes a cave formation that hangs down from the ceiling—Stalactite or Stalagmite?
Stalactite

14. What term describes the process in which fertile land turns dry due to droughts or exploitation of lands by human activity— Desertification or Drainage?
Desertification

15. What term is often used to describe an area of tropical grassland with widely scattered trees—Plateau or Savanna?
Savanna

16. The Beaufort Scale is used to grade what physical phenomenon?
Wind speed

17. What is the term used to describe grasslands in southern Africa—Steppe or Veld?
Veld

18. What term describes a wetland dominated by grasses—Marsh or Peat?
Marsh

19. What is the term for an area of low pressure with calm and light winds along the Equator where trade winds meet—Roaring Forties or Doldrums?
Doldrums

20. In an ocean, the region nearest to the land does not exceed 650 feet in depth. This region is known by what term—Beach or Continental Shelf?
Continental Shelf

21. What type of plant grows on another plant but does not get its nutrients from that plant—Parasite or Epiphyte?
Epiphyte

22. What is the name for an area that has a community of plants and animals characteristic of that area—Garden or Biome?
Biome

23. What term describes a scientist that specializes in the study of short-term weather—Meteorologist or Climatologist?
Meteorologist

24. What is the term for an area of low pressure with calm and light winds along the Equator where trade winds meet—Roaring Forties or Doldrums?
Doldrums

25. When a tornado forms over water, it may suck a column of water into the air. What is the term that describes this phenomenon—Storm Surge or Water Spout?
Water Spout

26. What term describes the amount of moisture in the air—
Humidity or Condensation?
Humidity

27. What term is used to describe a revolving tropical storm that
forms in the Pacific Ocean—Tornado or Typhoon?
Typhoon

28. What term describes the circulating whirlpools of surface cur-
rents driven by prevailing winds and the spinning motion of the
Earth—Gyres or Drains?
Gyres

29. What type of cloud characteristically produces precipitation—
Nimbus or Stratus?
Nimbus

30. What term describes a huge, bowl-shaped dent in the ocean
floor—Plain or Basin?
Basin

31. What type of volcano is formed over isolated areas of volcanic
activity where columns of magma rise through the seafloor—Hot
Spot Volcano or Stratovolcano?
Hot Spot Volcano

32. When seamounts sink as the seafloor beneath them subsides
and wave action results in a flattened summit, what type of sub-
merged mountain results—Guyot or Mound?
Guyot

33. The spin of Earth on its axis causes what phenomenon in which
weather systems lean towards the right of the line of travel
in the Northern Hemisphere and to the left in the Southern
Hemisphere—Coriolis Effect or Gulf Stream Effect?
Coriolis Effect

34. What term describes the solid layer of rock beneath the soil—
    Bedrock or Core?
    Bedrock

35. What term describes the process of obtaining fresh water from
    salt water—Desertification or Desalination?
    Desalination

36. What is the highest point of a wave—Crest or Crust?
    Crest

37. What is a small depression that forms when a chunk of ice that
    has been left in glacial till melts—Boulder or Kettle?
    Kettle

38. What is the term for a stream that flows into a larger stream like a
    river—Distributary or Tributary?
    Tributary

39. The boundary zone between the stratosphere and the meso-
    sphere is known as—Stratopause or Ionosphere?
    Stratopause

40. What is the term for a small, rapidly rotating wind that is made
    visible by the dirt it picks up—Hurricane or Whirlwind?
    Whirlwind

41. A commercially viable technology for the generation of electric-
    ity from nuclear power involves the splitting of atoms to obtain
    nuclear energy. What is this process called—fission or fusion?
    Fission

42. What describes a change in a substance from a liquid to a gaseous
    state—Evaporation or Condensation?
    Evaporation

43. What describes a change in a substance from a solid to a gaseous state—Sublimation or Condensation?
Sublimation

44. What term describes a sudden rise in water level in a river as a result of heavy rains—Flash Flood or Tsunami?
Flash Flood

45. What term describes a zone where warm and cold air meet and where there is hardly any noticeable movement of the air mass—Stationary Front or Jet Stream?
Stationary Front

46. What term describes a body of water that is smaller than a gulf and is partly enclosed by land—Bay or Lagoon?
Bay

47. What term describes a line that represents points on a topographic map with the same altitude—Isobar or Contour?
Contour

48. What type of map represents elevations—Geologic Map or Topographic Map?
Topographic Map

49. The symbols on a map that represent certain physical items are explained by a small table that accompanies these maps. What is this table called—Legend or Scale?
Legend

50. An isthmus is a narrow strip of land connecting a large landmass with which of the following—another large landmass or a large lake?
Another large landmass

51. Elements of nature consistently shape hills and ridges of sand in a desert. What term describes these hills and ridges—Arroyo or Dune?
Dune

52. Dark clouds that bring rain are called what—Nimbostratus or Cirrostratus?
Nimbostratus

53. Gneiss, marble, and slate are examples of what type of rock?
Metamorphic Rock

54. The Mariana Trench is the deepest trench in what large ocean?
The Pacific Ocean

55. What type of rock is associated with Earth's crust and magma?
Igneous Rock

56. Chalk and limestone are examples of what type of rock?
Sedimentary Rock

57. Which of the following contains a larger proportion of humus—swamp or dry soil?
Swamp

58. What term describes a cave formation that grows upward toward a ceiling of a cave—Stalactite or Stalagmite?
Stalagmite

59. The wind chill index combines air temperature and what other factor?
Wind Speed

60. What is the term for this aquatic ecosystem where fresh water from river meets salt water from sea?
Estuary

61. Long Island, Pamlico, and Puget are all examples of what physical feature?
Sound

62. Sand and gravel deposited in piles by a glacier or ice sheet is known by what term?
Moraine

63. A long, jagged ridge on the sea floor along the gap between two divergent tectonic plates is known as what?
Mid-Ocean Ridge

64. A thermometer is to temperature as an anemometer is to what?
Wind Speed

65. What is the term for a variety of hard, shiny coal that burns with little smoke and gives more heat than any other type of coal?
Anthracite

66. Bab-el-Mandeb, Palk, and Bass are examples of what type of physical feature?
Strait

67. What is the term for volcanic mudflow composed of pyroclastic material and water?
Lahar

68. Transform, Overthrust, and Reverse are types of what physical feature?
Faults

69. V-shaped valleys are formed by water. U-shaped valleys are formed by what type of physical feature?
Glaciers

70. What is the name given to the science of map making?
Cartography

71. Hills near the Yazoo River in Mississippi and the Palouse Hills of Washington are composed of loess, a sediment that is moved by what natural phenomenon?
Wind

72. What is the name of the very slow downward movement of soil and clay due to gravity, which can form distinctive talus cones at the bottom of steep inclines—Creep or Erosion?
Creep

73. What is the name of the phenomenon whereby supersaturated soil subjected to earthquakes loses its ability to hold the weight of buildings on it, causing the ground to momentarily behave like a liquid—Leaching or Liquefaction?
Liquefaction

74. What is the name for the petrified remains of prehistoric creatures that are often found in sedimentary rock—Hominids or Fossils?
Fossils

75. When glaciers or ice sheets flow into the ocean, they split in a process known as calving, creating what solid, floating masses of ice—Icebergs or Pack Ice?
Icebergs

76. What type of rock is more porous and can be found in an aquifer—Sandstone or Granite?
Sandstone

77. Today, gas drilling involves smashing through rock layers with columns of pressurized, chemically treated water to free underground gas. What is the term for this process—Hydraulic Fracturing or Hydraulic Cavitation?
Hydraulic Fracturing (Fracking)

78. The Salton Sea and the Caspian Sea are examples of lakes that are unusual in that they contain what substance?
Salt

79. The world's largest mass of limestone is in what large, treeless expanse located in Australia just north of the Great Australian Bight?
Nullarbor Plain

80. What is the name given to the valley formed on a fault by divergent plates—Graben or Horst?
Graben (Rift Valley)

81. Giant's Causeway in Ireland, a massive site with over 20,000 columns of basalt, an igneous rock, was formed by what process—Volcanism or Uplifting?
Volcanism

82. In contrast to felsic rocks that are rich in oxygen, aluminum, potassium, silicon and sodium, mafic rocks are commonly composed of magnesium and what other metal mined in the Mesabi Ranges?
Iron

83. Spectacular fjords, which dot the coasts of many Scandinavian countries, are formed when what large, moving masses of ice meet inlets of the sea?
Glaciers

84. Forests are cut down for planting crops or for grazing livestock. What term describes this process that enhances the greenhouse effect—Desertification or Deforestation?
Deforestation

85. What is the term for a substance that adds organic or inorganic plant nutrients to enrich the soil for increased productivity of crops?
Fertilizer

86. What is the lowest level of the atmosphere in which clouds and weather phenomena occur—Troposphere or Stratosphere?
Troposphere

87. What is the term for any gas that absorbs infrared radiation in the atmosphere and converts it into heat energy?
Greenhouse Gas

88. What is the most abundant greenhouse gas—Carbon Dioxide, Water Vapor or Methane?
Water Vapor

89. What term describes the collection and reprocessing of a resource so that it can be reused?
Recycling

90. What substance derived from coal is used as a fuel and as a reducing agent in smelting iron ore—Coke or Cacao?
Coke

91. What term describes the water from precipitation that flows over land and percolates into the ground—Stormwater Runoff or Groundwater?
Stormwater Runoff

92. What branch of agricultural science deals with principles and practices of soil, water and crop management—Agronomy or Horticulture?
Agronomy

93. Fresh snow reflects a higher percentage of radiation than glacial ice. Does fresh snow have a higher albedo or a lower albedo than glacial ice?
Higher albedo

94. The pH scale, a scale measuring acidity or basicity, ranges from 0 to 14, with 7 being neutral. What does a pH greater than 7 indicate—Acidity or Basicity?
Basicity

95. What is the term for the belt of fault lines and volcanoes encircling the Pacific Ocean—Ring of Fire or Ablation Zone?
Ring of Fire

96. What term describes a difference in elevation between any two points on a map?
Relief

97. During full moon and new moon, the sun and the moon are in line with one another. These are ideal conditions for which of the following—Spring Tides or Neap Tides?
Spring Tides

98. What do you call the horizontal angular difference between the True North and the Magnetic North—Magnetic Inclination or Magnetic Declination?
Magnetic Declination

99. What is name given to a fine-textured type of sedimentary rock formed principally from particles of clay?
Shale

100. What term relates to a piece of land adjacent to a body of water (e.g.: streams and rivers)—Watershed or Riparian?
Riparian

Physical Geography Terms

ACROSS

2. An underground layer of rock that contains water
5. The term for a flat area along the ocean floor: _____ plain.
7. An anemometer measures this (2 words, no spaces).
8. This term describes a bend in rock.
9. The lowest level of Earth's atmosphere where weather patterns develop is the _____.
11. A looping curve formed in a river as it winds through its path.
14. A line that connects areas on a map that have the same elevation known as a(n) _____ line.
16. The hot, solid layer between Earth's core and crust is known as the _____.
17. Term for the lines on a map indicating area of equal pressure.
18. The calm center of a hurricane.
19. A landform made of sediment that is deposited where a river flows into an ocean or lake is known as a(n) _____.

DOWN

1. The cold current that flows from Antarctica northwards along the west coast of South America is known as the Peru Current, or _____ Current.
2. A downward movement of snow, ice, and debris in a mountainous area is known as a(n) _____.
3. This type of lake is a crescent-shaped body of water that remains after a river carves a different path.
4. Tall, dark cloud known for producing thunderstorms.
6. A well in which water rises because of pressure within the aquifer is known as a(n) _____ Well.
10. The type of rock formed from volcanic activity: _____ rock.
12. A coastal inlet where fresh water mixes with salty ocean water is known by this term.
13. The specific rock from which oceanic crust is made.
15. The highest part of a wave is the _____

Physical Geography

Physical Geography, Part II

ACROSS

4. A front, or between two bodies of air, that stays in place
5. The point in the moon's orbit where it is closest to Earth
6. Precipitation that is a mixture of snow and rain and that comes down in sheets
10. The viscous layer between the crust and mantle
13. A structure formed by sand deposited where a bay joins a larger body of water
14. Soil that is composed of equal parts clay, sand, and silt
15. A rocky desert
16. A rocky ridge that is made up of a glacier's deposits
18. A series of rapids along a river
20. The layer of the atmosphere in which planes fly

DOWN

1. Wispy clouds found at high altitudes
2. The _____ scale measures the intensity of a tornado
3. A tornado that touches down on water
7. Hot winds that are common to southern California
8. A _____ map shows differences in altitude by use of texture
9. Erosion that is caused by wind
11. A wide, shallowly-sloped volcano with gentle streams of lava
12. An _____ tide takes place before a tsunami
17. A long, plunging valley at the bottom of the ocean
19. The altitude beyond which trees cease to grow

Physical Geography, Part II

Chapter 9

Cultural Geography

1. The Steelers are the football team of what industrial Pennsylvanian city located at the confluence of the Allegheny and Monongahela rivers?
Pittsburgh

2. Midsummer's Day is an important festival in what Baltic Sea country that has Öland as its second-largest island?
Sweden

3. The Sundance Film Festival is held in Park City in what western state that is also home to one of the largest salt lakes in the world?
Utah

4. The Mall of America, one of the largest shopping malls in the United States, is located near St. Paul and its twin city on the banks of the Mississippi River. Name this city.
Minneapolis

5. The Ice Festival is a major attraction in what Alaskan city on the Chena River in the Tanana Valley?
Fairbanks

6. The Indian Pueblo Cultural Center is located in what city in New Mexico?
Albuquerque

7. Haggis is a traditional sausage dish from what political unit of the United Kingdom that has Edinburgh as its capital?
Scotland

8. One can stroll down the Rue de Rivoli, view the Grande Arche in La Défense district, and peruse the galleries of the Louvre Museum in what Western European capital?
Paris

9. The hangi is a traditional meal of a native group that lives on the North and South Islands of a South Pacific nation. Name this native group.
Maori

10. The largest city in Louisiana is named after what French city that is closely associated with Joan of Arc, an important figure in the Hundred Years' War between Britain and France?
Orleans

11. The Canadian International Dragon Boat Race, the first of its kind outside Asia, is held annually in Canada's third largest city. Name this city that has the Burrard Inlet, the eastern arm of the Strait of Georgia.
Vancouver

12. The Anthem of Europe, Ode to Joy, was composed by Ludwig van Beethoven, who was born in the capital of the former West Germany. Name this major city in the North Rhine-Westphalia region.
Bonn

13. The Berlin Conference of 1884 served to carve up Africa and distribute it among the European powers, except for Ethiopia and which other country that has Monrovia as its capital?
Liberia

14. According to the belief of an Australian native group, the Dreamtime is the understanding of the world, of its creation, and its great stories. Name this native group.
Aborigines

15. The Dashiki is a garment often worn at celebrations in what oil-rich West African country whose Osun-Osogbo Sacred Grove, the cradle of Yoruba cultural traditions, is a World Heritage site?
Nigeria

16. The world's largest mounted statue of Ghengis Khan can be found in what country whose large nomadic people use gers as a primary shelter on the steppes?
Mongolia

17. Ur, located inland of the mouth of the Euphrates in Iraq, was a major city-state in ancient Sumer. Sumer was located in what region of the ancient world, known as "the land between the rivers"?
Mesopotamia

18. IJsselmeer, an enclosed inlet of the Atlantic Ocean, is in what European country famous for its tulips?
The Netherlands

19. Balboa Park, home to many museums and cultural institutions, is a major tourist attraction in what U.S. city just north of the Mexican border town of Tijuana?
San Diego

20. The Japanese, Chinese, and Korean cultures have ceremonies for the pouring and consumption of what popular beverage that is grown widely in areas like Darjeeling, India and Hangzhou, China?
Tea

21. The Defenestration of Prague was a major event that preceded the 30 Years War, a conflict between Catholicism and what other branch of Christianity, started by Martin Luther during the Reformation?
Protestantism

22. The Dutch built the fort of New Amsterdam on what U.S. island that was bought from the Delaware tribe for a legendary $24 in beads?
Manhattan

23. Bruschetta is a delicious appetizer consisting of toasted bread, raw garlic, and olive oil from a peninsular European country in the Mediterranean region. Name this country that has two independent countries within its borders.
Italy

24. Port Arthur and the Fremantle Prison were points of entry for convicts in a major British penal colony in the 19th century. Today, they are historic sites in which country?
Australia

25. Gorée Island, a historic site of slave holding and the African Renaissance Monument, a bronze representation of a man, woman and child emerging from a volcano, is located in what capital that is the westernmost in mainland Africa?
Dakar

26. The Treaty of Nanking was the conclusion of a series of wars between the Chinese and the British in the 1800s. Name these wars that were centered around and named for an addictive drug.
Opium Wars

27. Darien National Forest and Coiba National Park are in what country that split from Gran Colombia and is located on an S-shaped isthmus connecting the two American continents?
Panama

28. Caviar, regarded as an expensive delicacy in the West, forms a major part of the economy of many cities along the Caspian Sea in what country that is home to the ancient Achaemenid Empire?
Iran

29. What is the name given to the Chinese characters used in Japanese writing?
Kanji

30. Copacabana Beach and Corcovado Peak are tourist destinations in what Brazilian city famous for its Carnival Festival?
Rio de Janeiro

31. St. Lucia's Day, a day of feasting that is famous for its crown of candles, is celebrated in the largest and the most populous Scandinavian country. Name this country that is also home to the Smörgåsbord, an elaborate buffet.
Sweden

32. "Waltzing Matilda" is the most famous indigenous "Bush" song and is commonly associated with what continent that also boasts the Royal Flying Doctor Service, a major primary health care provider to rural and remote areas of its northeastern state?
Australia

33. Salsa, the Rumba, the Mambo, and the Cha-Cha-Cha are dances that originated in the largest country in the Greater Antilles. Name this country that is also famous for its tobacco plantations.
Cuba

34. Name the Southeast Asian country that is home to the imperial city of Hue and is also well-known for its floating markets on the Mekong River.
Vietnam

35. Which state, home to an extensive Navajo reservation and the Gila River, has the cities of Tucson and Phoenix and is part of what is often called the "Sun Belt"?
Arizona

36. What city on the Charles River is well-known as the cradle of the American Revolution and is home to the Red Sox professional baseball team?
Boston

37. The city of Rosario, originally a missionary station, is found west of the Rio de la Plata on the Parana River, in what country that is home to the world's widest avenue, Avenida 9 de Julio, and the famous Teatro Colón?
Argentina

38. Stone Mountain, the World of Coca-Cola, and the 1996 Olympics Park are all landmarks in what southern U.S. city that has the world's busiest airport, Hartsfield International?
Atlanta

39. The second-highest peak in the Cascade Range is revered by the local Native Americans. Name this peak, located in California.
Mt. Shasta

40. The Chapel in the Hills is a full-scale replica of Norway's Borgund Stave Church. This is in Rapid City in which U.S. state?
South Dakota

41. The 12th-century Kalon Minaret is a historic monument in the city of Bukhara in which Central Asian country?
Uzbekistan

42. Tulum, the site of ancient Mayan ruins, is an important stop for archaeologists visiting which Latin American country?
Mexico

43. Cairns is a town on the Coral Sea famous for its proximity to the Great Barrier Reef and for its sunny beaches. Cairns is located in what country?
Australia

44. Margarita Island and Lake Maracaibo are attractions in what South American country that is home to the Llanos and is located to the east of Colombia?
Venezuela

45. Salamanca and Cordoba are historical cities in what country that once ruled an empire that stretched from Canada to Chile?
Spain

46. Goa, Mozambique, Guinea-Bissau, and East Timor were all former colonies of what European power that also had a lasting influence on Brazil?
Portugal

47. Chapel of the Holy Cross is an attraction to the followers of Catholicism. This chapel is in the city of Sedona in which southwestern U.S. state?
Arizona

48. The Sinulog Festival, which takes place on the third Sunday in January in the city of Cebu, is held in honor of Jesus in the biggest Christian country in Asia. Name this country.
The Philippines

49. The petwo drums provide percussion for ethnic dances on a country on the island of Hispaniola that is influenced greatly by French culture. Name this country that has the historic city of Jacmel that was once a major export port for coffee and precious oils?
Haiti

50. The 2016 Summer Olympic Games will be held in which city that is famous for its Statue of Christ the Redeemer and Sugarloaf Mountain?
Rio de Janeiro

51. The Chukchi people, whose homeland is a peninsula of the same name, are the principal indigenous group of what large tundra in northeast Asia?
Siberia

52. The Mossi people hail from which landlocked country in Western Africa that has the city of Bobo Dioulasso and the origin of the three major tributaries of the Volta River?
Burkina Faso

53. The Golden Temple in Amritsar, India, is a holy site for followers of what religion?
Sikhism

54. The Torre de Belém, built during a country's colonial period, stands at the mouth of Lisbon's harbor. Name this country.
Portugal

55. Teruna Jaya ("the Victorious Youth") is a popular Balinese dance from which large archipelagic country?
Indonesia

56. Lutheranism is the primary denomination of Christianity that is practiced in what region of Europe?
Scandinavia

57. The caste system is a hereditary social class system that was once practiced by followers of what Asian religion?
Hinduism

58. Jeddah is the closest port city to which holy city that is said to be the birthplace of Islam?
Mecca

59. Ever since his exile, the Dalai Lama has ruled the autonomous region of Tibet from a monastery in Dharamsala in which country?
India

60. Yurts, circular tents of felt or animal skin, are used for shelter by nomads primarily in what landlocked Asian country?
Mongolia

61. Name the nomadic people in northern Africa that are called the "Blue People" because of the blue robes they wear.
Tuareg

62. If you are visiting the Czarist palaces and churches in the Kremlin, you are visiting which country?
Russia

63. The grave of Sheik Muhammed Ahmed can be found in the city of Omdurman. He was a national hero in which country south of Egypt?
Sudan

64. Ovambo is a language native to what country, formerly called German Southwest Africa, that contains the western edge of the Kalahari Desert?
Namibia

65. The Kojiki and the Nihongi are the sacred texts of which polytheistic religion indigenous to Japan?
Shintoism

66. Goulash is a stew of meat and vegetables, seasoned with paprika. This soup originated in which country whose largest lake is Lake Balaton?
Hungary

67. Oil wrestling, a sport where the two challengers are covered in oil before a fight, is a popular sport in a country that, in the Byzantine era, was home to the capital, Constantinople. Name this country.
Turkey

68. Bengali is the official language of which country that was once known as East Pakistan and contains the delta of the Ganges and Brahmaputra Rivers?
Bangladesh

69. Paella, a rice-based dish that contains shrimp, lemon, and other condiments, is native to what country on the Iberian Peninsula?
Spain

70. Samarkand, a major stop along the Silk Road, is now a city in a present-day country that is south of the rapidly shrinking Aral Sea. Name this country.
Uzbekistan

71. The book Unua Libro explains the foundations of what proposed universal language that is the most widely spoken constructed international auxiliary language?
Esperanto

72. Wangari Maathai, the first African woman and environmentalist to win the Nobel Prize, as well as Kenya's founding father Jomo Kenyatta, are from what ethnic group that is the largest in Kenya?
Kikuyu

73. Which southern African country is known as the "Rainbow Nation" because of its cultural diversity and its eleven official languages?
South Africa

74. Zapotec culture was centered in the present-day state of Oaxaca in which Latin American country?
Mexico

75. Arabic is the official language of which country that was the only one on the Mediterranean Sea to be colonized by Italy?
Libya

76. Though the people no longer wear them, klompen are shoes traditionally worn in a dance of the same name. These shoes are a symbol of what country bordering Belgium on the North Sea?
The Netherlands

77. St. Mark's Basilica and the Bridge of Sighs are major landmarks of which Italian city at the northern end of the Adriatic Sea?
Venice

78. The Imperial Palace of the Qing Dynasty, the last in China, is located within the walls of the Forbidden City, a residence for emperors in which present-day city?
Beijing

79. The archeological ruins of the ancient Mohenjodaro civilization can be found along the Indus River in the Sindh province of which country?
Pakistan

80. Catalan, Valencian and Galician are dialects spoken in which country that controls the colonies of Ceuta and Melilla on the Strait of Gibraltar.
Spain

81. The Boca Raton Museum of Art is a popular tourist attraction in which southeastern U.S. state?
Florida

82. The Mystic Seaport Museum is in which Northeastern U.S. state?
Connecticut

83. The Bennington Museum was founded in 1852 to commemorate the historic 1777 Revolutionary War Battle of Bennington in which Northeastern U.S. state?
Vermont

84. The Buffalo Bill Historical Center is in Cody in which western U.S. state?
Wyoming

85. The Historical Museum at Fort Missoula is in which western U.S. state?
Montana

86. Spanish architecture is most influenced by what North African people who invaded Spain and built structures like the Alhambra and cities like Cordoba?
Moors

87. Pottery and the widespread cultivation of silk are achievements attributed to the culture of what Asian country?
China

88. Dykes and windmills dot the countryside of what country that has the lowest elevation of the Benelux countries?
The Netherlands

89. Malagasy and French are spoken on what island nation in the Indian Ocean that is home to the ring-tailed lemur and other endangered species?
Madagascar

90. What Middle Eastern country, where the population is 39 percent Christian, has many significant Roman ruins in cities like Tyre and has a cedar tree on its flag?
Lebanon

91. A river in South America is named after a tribe known for its fierce women fighters in Greek mythology. Name this river.
Amazon River

92. Steel drums are a part of the rich musical heritage of what Caribbean country made up of two islands that is the southern-most in the Lesser Antilles?
Trinidad and Tobago

93. Hindustani is widely spoken in what Melanesian country, south-west of Wallis and Futuna Islands, famous for its beaches and coral reefs?
Fiji

94. El Yunque National Forest and the Arecibo Radio Telescope are points of interest in the largest US commonwealth. Name this commonwealth.
Puerto Rico

95. The Khmer people built the massive temple complex of Angkor Wat in a country what was once known as Kampuchea. What is the current name of this country on the Indochina Peninsula?
Cambodia

96. Mount Ararat, the purported site of Noah's Ark, is a religious site in what transcontinental country whose largest city has the Topkapi Palace?
Turkey

97. The Great Mosque of Djenné, the largest adobe structure in the world, was a major achievement of the ancient peoples of what country, famous for its cities of Timbuktu and Gao?
Mali

98. The Amarnath Caves, the site of a famous Hindu pilgrimage, are located in what disputed region between India, Pakistan, and China?
Kashmir

99. The Rock and Roll Hall of Fame on Lake Erie and the Pro Football Hall of Fame in Canton are two points of interest in what state that is home to the Cuyahoga Valley?
Ohio

100. The Tolstoy Museum is in the Tatarstan Republic of what country?
Russia

Cultural Geography

ACROSS

6. The natives in this U.S. Pacific island territory are called Chamorro and speak a language called Chamorro
7. The didgeridoo is an instrument traditionally played in this country
9. The _____ tribe is the predominant tribe in New Zealand
12. The largest Roman Catholic country in Asia
14. Wole Soyinka was a freedom fighter and Nobel Peace Prize Winner from this West African country
18. Pol Pot and the Khmer Rouge ruthlessly enforced Communism in this country
20. People of this nationality colonized East Timor

DOWN

1. The Hagia Sophia is a museum in this city that witnessed many different empires and religions
2. Hans Christian Andersen, who has written *The Ugly Duckling* and *the Emperor's New Clothes,* is from this country
3. Zen Buddhism influenced the concept of the tea ceremony in this island country
4. The Mambo is a fast-paced ballroom dance from this country
5. This script based on characters from Greek is used in writing Russian
8. The Dutch people in this country were known as "Afrikaners" or simply "Boers"
10. The balalaika is a stringed instrument from this country
11. The Running of the Bulls takes place at the San Fermin Festival in Pamplona in this country
13. Both Napoleon's and Hitler's troops marched through this French arch upon victory
15. They are called vaqueros in Mexico, gauchos in Argentina and _____ in English

16. To taste barbacoa and pozole, one would visit this Latin American country
17. Oktoberfest is a festival that was created to showcase Bavarian agriculture in this country
19. The birthplace of Islam and home of the Ka'aba

Cultural Geography

Chapter 10

Economic Geography

1.   Rubber is a major product exported from what country that occupies the southern part of the Malay Peninsula and the northern part of Borneo?
     Malaysia

2.   Which South American country that has Mendoza and Rosario as two of its largest cities is one of the world's largest per capita producers of beef?
     Argentina

3.   Name the European country on the Iberian Peninsula that is the world's largest producer of cork.
     Portugal

4.   Pitch Lake, known for its deposits of asphalt, is found in what Caribbean country off the east coast of Venezuela?
     Trinidad and Tobago

5.   The smallest independent South American country produces aluminum ingots for export. Name this country that was formerly known as Dutch Guiana.
     Suriname

6.   Most of the world's valuable amber, the fossilized resin of pine trees, is mined on the Baltic shores of what country whose border with the Russian exclave of Kaliningrad follows the path of the Neman River?
     Lithuania

7.   Most of the world's resins, including frankincense and myrrh, are found in what country that extends farthest south on the Arabian Peninsula?
     Yemen

8.   One of the world's largest gold deposits outside of Africa can be found on the island of Lihir. This island belongs to a nation that

has most of its territory on the largest landmass entirely within the Pacific. Name this nation and the landmass.
Papua New Guinea and the island of New Guinea

9. Name the country that is the world's second-largest producer of vanilla, and the world's largest producer of Ylang ylang, a fragrant tree used in manufacturing perfume?
Comoros

10. Name the country, with Zahedan and Tabriz as two of its major cities that is the third largest in the world in terms of proved oil reserves.
Iran

11. Organized trade of the sap of the acacia tree started in Sudan in 1820. Name the product that is formed from this sap.
Gum Arabic

12. Chittagong is the largest port of an Asian country that is the world's largest exporter of jute. Name this country on the Bay of Bengal.
Bangladesh

13. Name the country that was formerly called Serendib by Arab traders, and is now one of the largest tea exporters in the world.
Sri Lanka

14. One of the largest fishing fleets in the world can be found in what country that has the Chugoku Mountains and the Shinano River?
Japan

15. Which country is the leading exporter of rice in the world, ahead of Vietnam and China?
Thailand

16. Which European country with the regions of Flanders and Wallonia is home to Antwerp, the center of the world's diamond industry?
Belgium

17. Copper is mined in the mineral-rich province of Katanga, formerly called Shaba, in what African country that borders Rwanda and Angola?
Democratic Republic of the Congo

18. 95 percent of the world's supply of emeralds comes from a country that is also one of South America's leading gold producers. Name this country.
Colombia

19. Iron ore is mined in the Carajás Mine in Para, a state in which South American country?
Brazil

20. The eggs of sturgeon fish caught in the Caspian Sea are converted into caviar in Iran and in another country that spans two continents. Name this country.
Russia

21. Most of the rose oil that forms the base of perfumes comes from the Valley of Roses along the Maritsa River of which European country?
Bulgaria

22. Name the Caribbean country that is called the Isle of Spice because of the production of nutmeg in its hilly region.
Grenada

23. Name the country that is the third largest producer of uranium, behind Kazakhstan and Canada and is nicknamed the "Land Down Under" because of its location south of the Equator.
Australia

24. Which country south of St. Lucia is a leading grower of arrow-root, a source of starch used in medicines and flour?
St. Vincent and the Grenadines

25. The world's largest producer and exporter of platinum is also the second-largest producer of diamonds in Africa. Name this country whose northernmost point borders Zimbabwe.
South Africa

26. Which North American country is the third largest in the world in global beef exports?
United States

27. One of the biggest active gold mines in the Caribbean is in what island country that has Santo Domingo as its capital and has the Yaque River as its longest river?
Dominican Republic

28. The coalfields in the region of Silesia are one of the largest in the world. These fields are east of the Neisse River in which European country?
Poland

29. Which country that has Port Harcourt as the center of its oil industry is Africa's leading oil producer?
Nigeria

30. The desert of which long South American country that has the cities of Temuco and Valdivia is rich in mineral wealth?
Chile

31. Which country that borders both the Caspian Sea and the Barents Sea produces more than a quarter of the world's natural gas?
Russia

32. The United States' largest trading partner in sub-Saharan Africa is also the fourth-largest exporter of oil to the United States. Name this country.
Nigeria

33. MERCOSUR, a trading bloc, consists of Brazil, Argentina, Paraguay and what country that has an extensive gaucho culture in its Pampas region and has a short border with its former ruler Brazil?
Uruguay

34. The Ambassador Bridge connects what U.S. Rust Belt city on Lake St. Clair to Windsor, Canada?
Detroit

35. The Platte River flows through which city in Nebraska, home to stockyards and meat processing plants and situated just across the Missouri River from Council Bluffs, Iowa?
Omaha

36. The DAX is the stock exchange of which country that has most of its successful industrial centers on the Rhine River?
Germany

37. The world's largest producer of copra, the dried seed of the coconut that is used for its oil, is a country that lies across the Luzon Strait from Taiwan. Name this country.
The Philippines

38. The currency of an African country is named after a mine called the Witwatersrand. This mine is the source of over 40 percent of the world's gold in which country?
South Africa

39. Bauxite, or aluminum ore, is mined in which country, the only English-speaking country in the Greater Antilles?
Jamaica

40.   Manchester is a major textile manufacturing center in which European Union member country that refused the euro in favor of the pound?
United Kingdom

41.   Which of the following is not one of the Asian Tigers, a designation once given to four countries with strong economies— Hong Kong, Japan, South Korea, or Singapore?
Japan

42.   Cotton is the primary commercial crop farmed in the fertile Fergana Valley of which doubly landlocked Central Asian country?
Uzbekistan

43.   The world's largest producer of olives was the last major economy to emerge from the global recession in 2010. Name this country whose Tabernas Desert is the largest in Europe.
Spain

44.   Maquiladoras are foreign-operated factories in countries such as Mexico. The manufacturing and processing that take place there are activities that are considered to be on what level of industry – Primary or Secondary?
Secondary

45.   The Erie Canal, a manmade trench extending from Lake Erie in the west to the Hudson River in the east, is a significant passage for trade in which U.S. state?
New York

46.   Coffee is a major export of what Islamic country whose population is the fourth largest in the world?
Indonesia

47.   Name the city that is the largest manufacturing center in Canada.
Toronto

48. Tourism is the main industry of which Pacific island country to the north of New Zealand and east of Australia that is nearly a third Hindu?
Fiji

49. Potatoes originated in which country in the Andes that contains the Inca capital, Cuzco?
Peru

50. Magnetite is mined in the city of Magnitogorsk, which lies in what mountains in Russia?
Ural Mountains

51. Before the British opening of what canal in 1869 by the British did ships have to sail around the south of Africa, passing the treacherous Cape of Good Hope?
Suez Canal

52. Which U.S. state is a major producer of lumber—Washington or West Virginia?
Washington

53. The discovery of oil has replaced a country's noted for its pearl diving industry. Name this peninsular country on the Arabian Peninsula.
Qatar

54. Which U.S. state is a larger producer of blueberries—Maine or Montana?
Maine

55. Aside from the explosion of the reactors at the Fukushima Dai-ichi nuclear power plant, only one explosion has ever ranked as a 7 on the International Nuclear Event Scale. Name the Ukrainian city in which this took place.
Chernobyl

56. The Kiel Canal was built primarily for irrigation purposes in what country that borders the North Sea?
Germany

57. Brunei's main source of income is from oil that is mined from what body of water?
South China Sea

58. Mohair is a very soft material obtained from Angora goats. Angora goats are from which country whose capital was previously named for these goats?
Turkey

59. Serra Pelada, which means "Bald Mountain", is an extensive gold mine in the state of Para in which South American country whose southernmost point borders Uruguay?
Brazil

60. The world's largest producer of mica is a country that contains the third highest peak in the world. Name this Asian country.
India

61. What is Cameroon's largest port city, located on the Gulf of Guinea?
Douala

62. The "Black Belt" region in the American South is a region full of rich, black topsoil. The soil in this region dates back to the Cretaceous Period in Earth's history and can be found in which state?
Alabama

63. Most of the world's cobalt ore is mined in which African country whose main port is Matadi?
Democratic Republic of the Congo

64. Which mountain range in Minnesota is known for its output of iron ore?
Mesabi Range

65. Anshan is the main center of steel production in what country that is the U.S.'s second largest trading partner?
China

66. Norway's vast oil reserves can be attributed to its border with what body of water to its southwest?
North Sea

67. Roquefort cheese, which is made from the milk of sheep, is produced in what country that has the second largest economy in Europe?
France

68. What city located on the Elbe River is the primary shipbuilding center of Germany?
Hamburg

69. Anthracite, lignite, and limonite are types of what nonrenewable resource?
Coal

70. Which country known for its Longji Terraced Rice Fields in Guilin is the largest producer of tungsten in the world, producing 85 percent of the world's supply?
China

71. Name the largest producer of sugarcane in the Caribbean, a country that is also renowned for its cigars.
Cuba

72. According to the World Trade Association, which economic alliance is Russia's largest trading partner?
European Union

73. Which landlocked country in the Alps is famous for the export of cheese and chocolate as well as watches and other precision equipment?
Switzerland

74. The World Tourism Organization is a branch of the United Nations based in the capital of what southern European country whose language is the second most widely spoken in the world?
Spain

75. The world's largest producer of soybeans is a country that is the third largest in both area and population. Name this country.
United States

76. The kip is the currency of which landlocked country that was home to the French-occupied kingdom of Luang Prabang?
Laos

77. Rotterdam, the largest port city in the world, is located at the delta of the Rhine River in what country?
The Netherlands

78. Gold can be found in the Lena River basin in Siberia in what country?
Russia

79. Sericulture is a major industry in the Shandong Province of China. This is the harvesting of what material?
Silk

80. Which country that is the world's largest Portuguese speaking Catholic country is a top exporter of coffee, soybeans, beef, orange juice, and sugar?
Brazil

81. Which country is not one of the top five in global beef exports—Brazil, Canada, USA, Australia, or India?
Canada

82. Which country that owns the Chios Island is one of the European leaders in cotton production?
Greece

83. Which country is not in the top three in oil reserves and production in the Middle East—Saudi Arabia, United Arab Emirates, or Iraq?
United Arab Emirates

84. Which country is not a major producer of tea—India, Japan, or Myanmar?
Myanmar

85. Which country that has the Rosslare Harbor and the Connemara Peninsula uses peat, a partially decayed moss, as fuel?
Ireland

86. Wheat is the chief grain crop of which Asian country bordering Pakistan and Iraq that has the provinces of Khuzestan and West and East Azerbaijan?
Iran

87. Wood provides 70 percent of the fuel of which Asian country that has the Terai Valley as its breadbasket?
Nepal

88. What country that has Dhivehi as its main language mostly exports fish to Japan, Sri Lanka, and India?
Maldives

89. Which East Asian country that has the Inland Sea is the leader in automobile manufacturing?
Japan

90. Which island country directly south of Taiwan whose capital is known as the "Pearl of the Orient" is a leading exporter of coconuts and coconut oil?
Philippines

91. Gem-quality diamonds are a leading export in which African country that has the city of Oranjemund north of the mouth of the Orange River?
Namibia

92. Which country shares with Iran the world's largest gas field, the North Field, which is located in the Persian Gulf?
Qatar

93. Which founding NATO country was once the leader in automobile manufacturing, but now ranks fourth in the world?
USA

94. The Hindu Kush Mountains have been a source of rubies, silver and other mineral wealth such as lapis lazuli for thousands of years in which Asian country whose Wakhan Corridor borders China?
Afghanistan

95. The Chuquicamata Copper Mine is located northeast of Antofagasta in which country that has the largest GDP in southern South America?
Chile

96. In 2011, which country that has the cities of Brno and Ostrava had the highest GDP in Eastern Europe?
Czech Republic

97. Which country has the highest GDP of the OPEC countries in South America?
Venezuela

98. Which principality that was created by the union of the two states of Vaduz and Schulenburg has the highest GDP in Western Europe?
Liechtenstein

99. Although it is the smallest country in Central Africa, because of income from oil production, which country has the highest GDP in Central Africa?
Equatorial Guinea

100. Which country has the highest GDP in Northeast Africa?
Egypt

101. Which country in the Indian Ocean that has Victoria as its capital has the highest GDP in southern Africa?
Seychelles

102. Which country that has the world's largest open pit gold mine at Muruntau in the Qizilkum Desert is one of the top ten gold-producing countries?
Uzbekistan

103.   Which country is not a major automobile manufacturer—France, Japan, or China?
France

104.   United Parcel Service (UPS) operates Worldport, the largest fully automated package handling facility in the world, at Kentucky's largest city. Name this city.
Louisville

105.   Geothermal energy is larger source of power in which country— Iceland or Norway?
Iceland

Economic Geography

ACROSS

1. The name of the Russian stock exchange
4. Bolivia is one of the world's largest producers of this metal
7. The world's biggest producer of natural gas
11. Iron ore is plentiful in this range in Minnesota
12. Tagalog is one of the languages spoken in this country that is a major copra producer
14. Rich copper mines can be found in the Atacama Desert of this country
15. Major producer of natural rubber with the ringgit as its currency
16. The fertile Fergana Valley is a major cotton-producing region in this country
19. The African country south of Uganda that is a major producer of tea and coffee
20. The acronym for the body governing international trade

DOWN

2. The U.S. state that is a major avocado producer
3. The U.S. state with extensive diamond mines
5. Point Barrow, Alaska, has rich reserves of _____
6. Bauxite, also known as aluminum ore, can be found in this Greater Antilles country
8. The smallest of the four economic "Asian Tigers" in area
9. "The Steel City" is a center of heavy industry in Pennsylvania
10. Coal mines are scattered throughout the Silesia region of this country
13. The world's third largest producer of gold
17. The port that serves Sao Paulo
18. Once plentiful phosphate reserves on this Pacific island country with a capital of Yaren were depleted in the last decade.

Economic Geography

Chapter 11

Further Study

1. Wildfires are more prevalent in which state—Kansas or California?
   California

2. Hurricanes are more prevalent in which state—Mississippi or Oregon?
   Mississippi

3. Earthquakes are more prevalent in which state—California or Alaska?
   Alaska

4. Which part of United States has the greater population density—West Coast or Midwest?
   West Coast

5. Which state has counties with a higher Asian population—Oregon or Florida?
   Oregon

6. Which U.S. state has a larger Hispanic population—Colorado or Louisiana?
   Colorado

7. Which state has a higher wind energy potential—Kansas or North Carolina?
   Kansas

8. Which state has a higher geothermal potential—Washington or Ohio?
   Washington

9. Which state has a higher solar energy potential—New Mexico or Missouri?
   New Mexico

10. Which state has a higher biomass potential—Wisconsin or Alaska?
Wisconsin

11. Which northeastern state extends farther south—Delaware or Maryland?
Maryland

12. Which U.S. state extends farther west—Pennsylvania or New York?
Pennsylvania

13. Which U.S. state extends farther north—North Dakota or Minnesota?
Minnesota

14. Which U.S. state extends farther east—Massachusetts or Maine?
Maine

15. Which is the westernmost U.S. territory—Midway Island or Howland Island?
Midway Island

16. Which is the easternmost U.S. territory—Jarvis Island or Wake Island?
Wake Island

17. Which is the northernmost U.S. territory—Northern Mariana Islands or Puerto Rico?
Northern Mariana Islands

18. Which is the southernmost U.S. territory—Jarvis Island or American Samoa?
American Samoa

19. Two guides from the Lewis and Clark Expedition were voyageurs, or French-Canadian hunter-traders, in these Mandan villages. The Knife River Indian Villages Historic Site lies on the former site of the Mandan Village in which present-day state?
North Dakota

20. The Lewis and Clark Expedition built a log cabin named Fort Clatsop in Astoria in which U.S. state?
Oregon

21. During their return journey, Lewis and Clark took separate routes. Clark followed what river to reach the Missouri River?
The Yellowstone River

22. As part of the Missouri Compromise of 1820 that stipulated an equal number of slave states and "free" states, when the slave state of Missouri joined the Union, which New England state joined the Union as a "free" state?
Maine

23. Bastille Day is a national holiday that commemorates the storming of the Bastille Prison that took place on July 14, 1789. Bastille Day is celebrated in what country?
France

24. Which eastern Mediterranean country bordering Bulgaria and Armenia is a NATO member but not a member of the European Union?
Turkey

25. Following an earlier 2008 referendum, self-rule was introduced in a Danish island that is about 81% ice-capped. Name this island.
Greenland

26. Name the British Overseas territory about 648 miles east of Cape Hatteras, North Carolina.
Bermuda

27. Name the only Balkan country bordering Austria and Italy that has a very short coastline on the Adriatic Sea.
Slovenia

28. The city of Bilbao, well-known for its Guggenheim Museum, is in the Basque Region of what country?
Spain

29. Name the waterway linking the Atlantic Ocean with the Pacific and separating mainland Chile from Tierra del Fuego.
Strait of Magellan

30. The Strait of Magellan, which separates Patagonia from Tierra Del Fuego, is in what continent?
South America

31. The Balkan Peninsula is located in which continent?
Europe

32. The Mato Grasso Plateau is in what continent?
South America

33. The Galapagos Islands on the Pacific belong to which country that has Guayaquil as its largest city?
Ecuador

34. The walled city of Harar, considered by many Muslims to be the fourth "Holy City" following Mecca, Medina, and Jerusalem is located in which landlocked country that borders Kenya and Somalia?
Ethiopia

35. The Prut River forms the border between Romania and which landlocked country to its east?
Moldova

36. In 2016, which city in South America will be the first to host the Olympics?
Rio de Janeiro

37. Which Mid-Atlantic city is known for its steel production in the United States?
Pittsburgh

38. Casiquiare Channel connects the Amazon-Negro River system to which major river in Venezuela?
The Orinoco River

39. Name the world's second-largest continent in both area and population.
Africa

40. Which country bordering Cameroon and Gabon is Sub-Saharan Africa's third largest oil exporter?
Equatorial Guinea

41. A gelatinous fish, found off of Bahia coast in the Atlantic Ocean, may be a known member of a group of mysterious bottom-dwellers known as jellynose fish. Bahia is in what large country in the Western Hemisphere?
Brazil

42. In October 2009, a thirty-three-foot-wide "Blue Stonehenge" was discovered just over a mile from the original Stonehenge near what city in United Kingdom?
Salisbury

43. The easternmost point of Afghanistan borders Tajikistan and what other country?
China

44. Seine, Rhine and Rhone are major rivers in what country in Western Europe?
France

45. A dredging company recently discovered a U.S. tank from World War II near the mouth of the Pasig River in which Southeast Asian country?
The Philippines

46. Name the Russian Republic west of Chechnya and to the east of North Ossetia that has Magas as its capital?
Ingushetia

47. In 451 AD, the Franks joined the Romans to defeat Attila the Hun at the battle of Chalons. Chalons is in what present-day country?
France

48. Algarve coast is to Portugal as Costa Blanca is to what?
Spain

49. Sheep that are raised for wool and meat outnumber people in what country that borders the Foveaux Strait?
New Zealand

50. The northernmost point in mainland Asia is Cape Chelyuskin, Russia. This cape is part of what peninsula that lies between the Kara Sea and Laptev Sea.
Taymyr Peninsula

51. Though Bougainville is the largest island in the Solomon Islands archipelago in Melanesia, it belongs to what country that shares New Guinea with Indonesia?
Papua New Guinea

52. Which state is a major producer of iron ore—Minnesota or New Mexico?
Minnesota

53. Name the largest sea in the world.
The Coral Sea

54. Swakopmund and Walvis Bay are coastal cities in what African country that has the Etosha Pan near its border with Angola?
Namibia

55. A deep hollow in the mountains carved out by the head of a glacier is knows as what?
Cirque

56. Burgas, on the Black Sea, is a major port in which European country dominated by the Balkan Mountains?
Bulgaria

57. The city of Darwin is on the Timor Sea in which continent—Australia or South America?
Australia

58. Name the ridge that is also the longest mountain range in the world.
Mid-Atlantic Ridge

59. The deepest point of the Mariana Trench is called what?
Challenger Deep

60. The city of Bergen, on the Atlantic, is located in which European country?
Norway

61. If there is an 80% or greater chance that the temperature is expected to fall to 32 degrees (F) or lower in the next 3 to 30 hours, what type of warning will your weather station issue—A Freeze Warning or a Frost Advisory?
Freeze Warning

62. What term describes a Mediterranean wind that blows north from the Sahara Desert, reaching very high speeds in North Africa and Southern Europe?
Sirocco

63. Which is a major port city in India—New Delhi or Mumbai?
Mumbai

64. What island group in Indonesia was once known as the "Spice Islands"?
Molucca Islands

65. In September 2011, a forest fire near the Canadian town of Fort McMurray resulted in the closure of highways in the region. Fort McMurray is in which Canadian province?
Alberta

Chapter 12

Mock Bee

Preliminary Competition

Round 1: United States Geography

Questions in Round 1 focus on the geography of the United States.

1. The Ozark Plateau and the Ouachita Mountains meet near which city—Little Rock or St. Louis?

2. The Brooks Range and Prudhoe Bay are located in which state—California or Alaska?

3. The John F. Kennedy Space Center is located in which city—Cape Canaveral or Washington, D.C.?

4. Which state produces more peanuts than any other state—Georgia or Utah?

5. Tornados have often caused damage in which state—Kansas or Wyoming?

6. The Confederate Memorial at Stone Mountain is located in which state—North Dakota or Georgia?

7. The third largest reef system in the world is found in which state—California or Florida?

8. The USS Arizona Memorial is found in which state—Arizona or Hawaii?

9. Oswego, New York, is on which lake—Lake Erie or Lake Ontario?

10. The city of Bismarck is on which river—Columbia or Missouri?

11. The Willamette Valley is in which state—New Jersey or Oregon?

12.   Which capital city is located on the North Canadian River—Madison or Oklahoma City?

13.   Which state averages more inches of rainfall per year—Nevada or Alaska?

14.   Lake Powell is a major tourist destination in which state — Minnesota or Utah?

15.   Which state is the largest producer of cheese—Wisconsin or Iowa

Round 2: U.S. Cities

Questions in Round 2 may be based on the United States.

1.   Settlers from western Massachusetts founded the city of Fort Dummer, now a state park, near the present-day city of Brattleboro. Fort Dummer was the first white settlement in which state—Vermont or Maine?

2.   The Shoshone Falls is about 5 miles from Twin Falls on the Snake River in which state that has Lake Pend Oreille in its panhandle region—Texas or Idaho?

3.   Titusville and New Smyrna Beach are important sites for nature lovers in the Canaveral National Seashore in which state—Georgia or Florida?

4.   The Lowell Observatory is in the city of Flagstaff in which state—New Mexico or Arizona?

5.   In the early 1680s, a group of Quakers under William Penn set sail for America and later settled in a region to the west of the Delaware River thereby establishing which state—Delaware or Pennsylvania?

6.   Cooperstown, home of the Baseball Hall of Fame, is in which state—Massachusetts or New York?

7. Medford, a point of entry to Crater Lake National Park, is located in which state—Oregon or Vermont?

8. Located in the foothills of the Blue Ridge Mountains, Spartanburg is a distribution center for peaches in which state—South Carolina or South Dakota?

9. The Springer Mountain, in the Chattahoochee National Forest, at the endpoint of the Appalachian Trail, is in which state—Maine or Georgia?

10. The Manassas National Battlefield site is in which state—Maryland or Virginia?

11. The Del Rio International Bridge in Del Rio is a major land border port of entry in which state—California or Texas?

12. The city of Vicksburg, at the confluence of the Mississippi and the Yazoo Rivers, is in which state—Mississippi or Louisiana?

13. Parris Island is a Marine Corps Recruit Depot near Beaufort in which state—California or South Carolina?

14. Pago Pago, in the Pacific Ocean, is a major city in which U.S. territory—Guam or American Samoa?

15. Ponce is the second largest city in which U.S. political territory—Puerto Rico or the U.S. Virgin Islands?

Round 3: U.S. City Comparison

In Round 3 the student may be asked questions that compare two cities in the United States.

1. Which city is situated on a panhandle—Jackson, Mississippi; Amarillo, Texas; or Huntsville, Alabama?

2.   Which city is located on a major river—Madison, Wisconsin; Provo, Utah; or Shreveport, Louisiana?

3.   Which city is closest to Salton Sea— Salt Lake City, Utah; Macon, Georgia; or San Diego, California?

4.   Which city has a major oceanographic institution—Woods Hole, Massachusetts; Chattanooga, Tennessee; or Kansas City, Missouri?

5.   Which city is located at a lower elevation—New Orleans, Louisiana; Nashville, Tennessee; or Spokane, Washington?

6.   Which city is in the Mountain Time Zone—Pierre, South Dakota; Las Vegas, Nevada; or Tucson, Arizona?

7.   Which city is on the Missouri River—Omaha, Nebraska; Davenport, Iowa; or Springfield. Missouri?

8.   Which city gets more snow during winter—Tacoma, Washington; Beaverton, Oregon; or Syracuse, New York?

9.   Which city is located closer to the Gulf of Mexico—Corpus Christi, Texas; Baton Rouge, Louisiana; or Gainesville, Florida?

10.   Which city is closer to the historic Appalachian Trail—Casper, Wyoming; Roanoke, Virginia; or Memphis, Tennessee?

11.   Which city has a larger Latino population—Denver, Colorado; Concord, New Hampshire; or Salt Lake City, Utah?

12.   Which city is more likely to be affected by the landfall of a hurricane—Los Angeles, California; Boston, Massachusetts; or Gulfport, Mississippi?

13.   Which city has the National Football Hall of Fame—Boston, Massachusetts; Dallas, Texas; or Canton, Ohio?

14.   Which city lies north of the Arctic Circle—Prudhoe Bay, Alaska; Seward, Alaska; or Bangor, Maine?

15.   The Huntington Tri-State Airport is located in which city— Huntington, West Virginia; Huntington Beach, California; or Huntington, Indiana?

Round 4: Odd Item Out

In this round, the student will be given a choice of three answers. The student chooses the one answer that does not belong.

1.   Which country does not include at least a small section of the Himalayas – Bhutan, Mongolia, or Nepal?

2.   The Nile River does not pass through which country—Sudan, Senegal, or Egypt?

3.   Which country is not predominantly Catholic—Philippines, Russia, or Mexico?

4.   Which country is not landlocked—Lesotho, Serbia, or Uruguay?

5.   Which country is not crossed by the Equator—Equatorial Guinea, Gabon, or Kenya?

6.   Which country does not have any territory that once belonged to the Portuguese—India, Brazil, or Thailand?

7.   Which country does not have tropical rain forests—Nigeria, Saudi Arabia, or Brazil?

8.   Which country does not border France—Germany, Portugal, or Spain?

9.   Which country is not heavily populated—Bangladesh, Mongolia, or Indonesia?

10. Which country is not on the Indian Ocean—Kenya, Nigeria, or Australia?

11. Which country does not border the Mediterranean—Turkey, Lebanon, or Iraq?

12. Which country is not very mountainous—Afghanistan, Austria, or Bangladesh?

13. Which is the only African country separated from Madagascar by a channel of the same name as that of the country— Mozambique, Tanzania, or Zimbabwe?

14. Which country does not border Iraq—Syria, Iran, or Lebanon?

15. Which country does not border Guatemala—Mexico, Honduras, or Nicaragua?

Round 5: Continents

In this round, the competition starts branching out to other parts of the world.

1. Which continent has the Ungava Peninsula?

2. Mt. Damavand is the highest peak in a country on the Caspian Sea in which continent?

3. Tobruk and Benghazi are well-known Mediterranean cities on which continent?

4. The Uluru Peak is a major tourist site near the city of Alice Springs on which continent?

5. The Pantanal, the world's largest freshwater wetland, lies mostly in the largest country on what continent?

6. The historic city of Cusco is on what continent that has the world's longest mountain range?

7. The world's major religions originated on what continent?

8. Callao and Santos are port cities on which continent?

9. The capital city of Moscow is on which continent?

10. The Volta River is a major lifeline for many countries on which continent?

11. The Burgundy region, well-known for its wines, is on which continent?

12. The Empty Quarter, known as Rub' al-Khali, is a long span of desert on which continent?

13. The Apennines form the backbone of a historic country on which continent?

14. The Jura Mountains and the Jutland Peninsula are both located on which continent?

15. The McMurdo Sound and the Bellingshausen Sea are located on which continent?

Round 6: World's Rivers

1. Nantes and Orleans are major cities on which French river?

2. Livingston is city on which great African river?

3. Toledo, Spain, is located on what river?

4. Baghdad, Iraq, is on what river?

5.   Florence, Italy, is on what river?

6.   N'Djamena, Chad, is on what river?

7.   The historic German city of Dresden is on what river?

8.   Zhengzhou, China, is on what river?

9.   Patna, India, is on what river?

10.   Hanoi, Vietnam, is on what river?

11.   Novi Sad, Serbia, is on what river?

12.   Zagreb, Croatia, is on what river?

13.   Nizhniy Novgorod, Russia is on what river?

14.   Yakutsk, in Asian Russia, is on what river?

15.   Ciudad Guayana, Venezuela, is on what river?

Round 7: Physical Geography

1.   What would you call a group of islands—An archipelago or Coral reefs?

2.   What would you call a semi-arid grassland along the southern border of Africa's Sahara Desert—Prairies or Sahel?

3.   An escarpment is a cliff that separates flat areas of land lying where—At the same elevation or At different elevations?

4.   A narrow body of water that links two larger bodies of water is—an Isthmus or a Strait?

5.   The mantle is a thick layer of Earth's interior that lies between the crust and the—Nucleus or Core?

6.   In the hot dry desert regions of the earth, underground water tends to support pockets of vegetation growth. These pockets are known as—Lichens or Oases?

7.   A transform boundary is a place where two plates slip past each other—moving in opposite directions or same direction?

8.   Plate tectonics is a scientific theory that states that pieces of Earth's lithosphere are in motion, driven by convection currents in the—core or the mantle?

9.   Harry Hess, an American geologist, gave what name to the process that continuously adds new material to the ocean floor—seafloor spreading or subduction?

10.   Earth's most recent era is known as—Mesozoic or Cenozoic?

11.   The three main types of freshwater wetlands are marshes, swamps and regions commonly formed in depressions left by melting ice sheets several thousands of years ago. Name these regions—Gully or Bog?

12.   Chemicals used to kill insects that damage crops are known as—Dioxin or Pesticides?

13.   Water that is partly fresh and partly salty where mangrove trees grow well is known as—Brackish Water or Soft Water?

14.   What happens to air pressure as altitude increases—does it decrease or does it remain the same?

15.   What term describes the boundary on which a warm front has been overtaken by a cold front that also brings precipitation—Occluded Front or Cold Front?

At this point, the competition needs to have the ten finalists. If there is a tie, tie-breaker questions may be applied. The questions are read twice and no questions or clarifications are allowed. The topics could cover anything related to geography.

Final Competition (Double-Elimination)

This is a double-elimination round. The student who misses two_questions is excused from the competition.

The Society will not accept "Holland" as a synonym for the country "Netherlands," and "England" for the country "United Kingdom of Great Britain and Northern Ireland," as England is a political division. Shortened forms of country names are acceptable, such as "United Kingdom," "Great Britain," or "Britain" for "United Kingdom of Great Britain and Northern Ireland." The National Geographic Society recognizes Europe and Asia as two continents. Oceania is considered a region rather than a continent, but Australia is a continent. In addition, the National Geographic Society recognizes four oceans—Arctic, Atlantic, Indian, and Pacific. The Southern Ocean, found in many maps, is not accepted.

Final round

Moderator says: The first set of Final Round questions may involve a map. Here, we have a map that shows provinces, territories, and capital cities in Canada. Each participant will get a separate question. Each participant uses the information on the map to answer your question. The student has 15 seconds to answer. Questions are asked in turn.

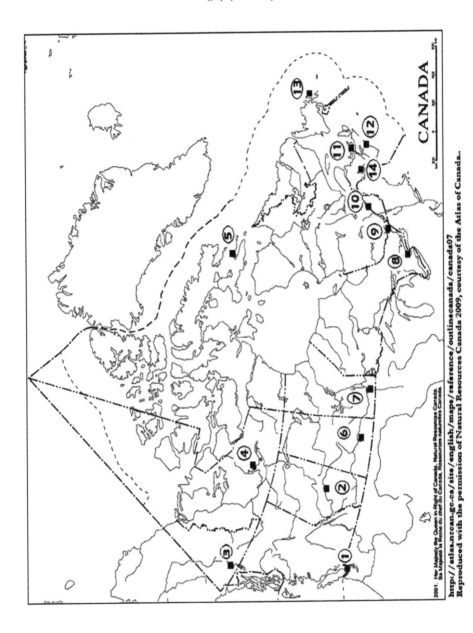

1. Saskatchewan is the largest producer of potash in Canada. Give the number and name of its capital city.

2. The most populous city in the Yukon Territory is also its capital. Give the number and name of this city.

3. Give the number and name of the capital city of Nunavut, Canada's newest territory.

4. The Golden Horseshoe in Ontario is one of the most populated regions in Canada. Give the number and name of its capital city.

5. Calgary is one of the major cities of Alberta. Give the name and number of Alberta's capital city.

6. The Churchill and the Nelson Rivers are important rivers in Manitoba. Give the number and name of its capital city.

7. New Brunswick's major port city is on the Bay of Fundy. Give the number and name of its capital city.

8. Prince Edward Island is Canada's smallest province. Give the number and name of its capital city.

9. Happy Valley-Goose Bay is an important city in Newfoundland and Labrador. Give the number and name of Newfoundland and Labrador's capital city.

10. Canada's largest province has the same name as its capital city. Give the number and name of this city.

11. Cape Breton Island belongs to Nova Scotia. Give the number and name of its capital city.

12. Give the number and name of Canada's capital city.

Written Round: Next, students may be asked to respond to the next question/questions by writing an answer on the sheet of paper provided.

13.   The Tallgrass Prairie National Preserve is in which state?

At this point, the moderator may revert back to oral questions.

14.   Selma, a city well-known for its historic "Selma to Montgomery marches," is in what state bordering Florida and Mississippi?

15.   The Marsh-Billings-Rockefeller National Historic Park is easily accessible from Woodstock in which New England state that was an independent country from 1777 to 1791?

16.   The Russell Cave Monument, home to prehistoric people for more than 10,000 years, is near to which US state's border with Tennessee?

17.   The Delaware Water Gap National Recreation Area borders Pennsylvania and what state that has the Barnegat Bay on the Atlantic?

18.   The Stellwagen Bank National Marine Sanctuary lies off the coast of what state that owns the Nantucket Island?

19.   The Gulf Islands National Seashore spans Florida and what other state?

20.   The Haleakala National Park is located near Kula on which Hawaiian island?

21.   The grounds of Pipestone National Monument are sacred to Native Americans. This is located in which state that has Duluth as the westernmost deep-water port on the St. Lawrence Seaway?

22.   The Lassen Volcanic National Park is accessible from the town of Mineral in what state?

The National Geographic Society will have a longer list of questions. The school conductors are not going to run out of questions.

Championship Round

Only two finalists will emerge from the previous competition. They will be competing with a clean slate. The Championship Round consists of three questions. Whoever correctly answers the most questions in the set of three becomes the school. The moderator will read the question twice and no questions are entertained. This is a written round.

1. In 2011, the principal port city of Latakia was the scene of violence in a major uprising in what Eastern Mediterranean country?

2. The Sirmilik National Park of Canada represents the Northern Eastern Arctic Lowlands Natural Region and portions of the Lancaster Sound Marine Region. This is located on what island?

3. Mount Wilson Observatory, in the San Gabriel Mountains, was under high alert when, in August 2009, wildfires threatened what national forest in California?

Championship Tiebreaker Questions

If there is a tie at the end of the Championship Round, the Society will have a set of tiebreaker questions and the champion is decided using a single-elimination procedure.

Again, this is written round. The moderator will read the question twice and there are no repeats allowed. It is quite possible that some of the questions may not have enough clues. This is true if the tie-breaker rounds last for a long time.

1.   Lake Van is located in which Eastern Mediterranean country bordering Georgia and Iran?

2.   The Christiansted National Historic Site is located on the southernmost of the three major islands in the U.S. Virgin Islands territory. Name this island.

3.   Name the most northerly national forest in the U.S.

4.   The Orange River rises in the Drakensberg Mountains of which small country in southern Africa?

5.   The Gallatin River is a tributary of what U.S. River?

6.   The Rodin Museum is located in which city in Pennsylvania?

Contributions from Past Participants

1. The Gulf of Gabes prominently features into the coastline of which country?
    Tunisia

2. Sharm al Sheikh is a resort town on which body of water?
    Red Sea

3. Which Brazilian state was formerly a country?
    Acre

4. Sort these 4 rivers from north to south: Severn, Albany, Churchill, Nelson.
    Churchill, Nelson, Severn, Albany

5. Lubeck, a city formerly part of the Hanseatic League, is on which river?
    The Trave River

6. American Falls Reservoir, located west of Pocatello is in the Snake River Plain of which US state?
    Idaho

7. Which lake, the largest in North Dakota is situated along the course of the Missouri River and was named for a famous Native American?
    Lake Sakakawea

8. This river, described as the dividing line between the Old South and New Southwest forms part of the border between Texas and Louisiana and comes from the Spanish word for "cypress". Name this river.
    Sabine River

9. The Apostle Islands belong to a state that has the town of Superior as its largest port on the lake by the same name. Name the state that owns the Apostle Islands and has the city of Superior.
    Wisconsin

10. The Monongahela and Allegheny Rivers merge in what major industrial city to form the Ohio River?
Pittsburgh

11. The 1842 Webster-Ashburton Treaty created a border between New Brunswick and which U.S. state?
Maine

12. In the Adams-Onis Treaty of 1819, ratified in 1821, Spain ceded which present-day state at the southeastern extreme of the forty-eight contiguous states?
Florida

13. The first major battle of the Civil War ended in a surprising Union defeat. Name this 1861 battle.
First Battle of Bull Run (or First Manassas)

14. The Women's Rights Movement in the United States started with the Seneca Falls Convention in which state?
New York

15. Name the agreement passed in 1820 that called for the abolishment of slavery in all territories north of 36' 30".
Missouri Compromise

16. What Asian country that has Busan as its second-largest city is also known as "The Land of the Morning Calm"?
South Korea

17. A major Russian river, with the major industrial cities of Novosibirsk and Khanty-Mansiysk on its banks, empties into a gulf east of the Yamal Peninsula. Name this river.
Ob River

18. The Battle of Talas was fought near the border of modern day Kazakhstan and Kyrgyzstan between the Abbasid Caliphate and the Tang Dynasty that effectively ended a country's expansion

into central Asia and marked the beginning of the decline of the Tang empire. Name this country.
China

19. Which archipelagic country has Luganville as its second largest city and Espiritu Santo as its largest island?
Vanuatu

20. The Battle of Austerlitz, one of Napoleon's greatest military victories, was fought in what present day country that has the Charles Bridge in its capital?
Czech Republic

21. Name the treaty signed on December 21, 1814, named for a city in modern day Belgium that effectively ended the War of 1812.
Treaty of Ghent

22. Name the largest province in Panama, with its largest city at La Palma, which contains the only gap in the Pan American Highway.
Darien

23. The controversial American military base at Futenma is located on the northeast corner of what Japanese island whose largest city is Naha?
Okinawa

24. What major city in Northeast Africa is home to a significant minority of Coptic Christians?
Cairo

25. Name the city located on the Mountain Nile River that is the capital of the country of South Sudan.
Juba

26. Name the German city located on the Main River that is the country's financial capital.
Frankfurt

27. Which Portuguese-speaking country is the largest oil producer in sub-saharan Africa?
Angola

28. What Dutch city is one of the world's largest ports?
Rotterdam

29. What Moroccan city, known as the Red City, was once one of the most important imperial cities in the nation?
Marrakech

30. What Chinese city, capital of the Xinjiang province, is the commercial and cultural hub in northwestern China?
Urumqi

31. What city in the West Bank serves as the de facto headquarters of the Palestinian Authority?
Ramallah

32. What Greek island was the center of the ancient Minoan civilization?
Crete

33. What country, located west of Madagascar, is known for being home to the now-extinct dodo bird ?
Mauritius

34. The Frankincense Trail, in important route for ancient incense trading and an UNESCO World Heritage Site, is located in what country?
Oman

35. The source of which river, the main tributary of the Niger River, is in the Adamawa Plateau of northern Cameroon?
The Benue River

36. Name the shallow inland gulf that separates Trinidad and Tobago from Venezuela.
The Gulf of Paria

37. Rome is to the Tiber River as Riga is to what?
Daugava River (or Western Dvina River)

38. Jau National Park is to Brazil as West Lunga National Park is to what?
Zambia

39. Nuku'alofa, the capital of Tonga, is located on which island?
Tongatapu

40. The capital of the autonomous region of Abkhazia is a port, rail junction and a holiday resort on the eastern coast of the Black Sea. Name this city.
Sukhumi

41. World's largest Loess Plateau is primarily in which Chinese province that has Xi'an as its capital—Henan or Shaanxi?
Shaanxi

42. Jefferson City was built at the confluence of the Missouri and which other river?
The Osage River

43. Ogaden is a region primarily in which African country bordering Eritrea?
Ethiopia

44. What river forms the western border of Liechtenstein?
The Rhine River

45. Marseille, France, is on what body of water?
Gulf of Lion

The format of the questions in Mr. Iyer's Geography Bee Demystified resemble closely to the types of questions that are found at different levels of the Geo Bee competition. I would recommend this book as one of the supplements in your preparation.
Stefan Petrovic, third-place winner, 2011-2012 National Geographic Bee

****

Geography Bee Demystified not only gave me superb test questions and topics, but it also saved me hours in studying by guiding me into the right subject areas.
Luke Hellum, top-ten finalist, 2011-2012 National Geographic Bee

****

Mr. Iyer's guides contain information that will not only prepare one to compete successfully at the National Geographic Bee, but also to extend one's knowledge of our ever-changing world.
Arjun Venkataraman, Ohio second-place winner, 2010

****

Some of the questions in this section are contributed by
Spencer Seballos, Ohio second-place winner, 2008

****

"The questions within this book (Geography Bee Demystified) are rigorous and require a dedicated student to spend many hours preparing for stiff competition."
Sebastian Albu in All News, Book Reviews, Education News, Blogger News Network

****

"This (*Geography Bee Demystified*) is a great resource that helped me prepare for the National Geography Bee after winning the New Hampshire State Geography Bee."
Milan Sandhu, The 2007 and 2008 New Hampshire champion and the 2008 top-ten finalist

****

"The *Geography Bee Demystified* is an excellent resource—a must read—for all those preparing for the National Geography Bee. Its comprehensive coverage allows one not only to prepare for the competition, but also to apply the knowledge gained for use in future studies in Geography, World Cultures and Earth Sciences."
Nikhil Desai, The 2008 California champion and the 2008 top-ten finalist at the Nationals

****

The questions put you through the thought process needed for answering those tough questions.
Arjun Kandaswamy (The 2009 Nationals second-place winner)

****

Geography Bee Simplified and Demystified are good books for kids preparing for the bee with challenging questions.
Zaroug Jaleel (The 2009 Massachusetts champion and the Nationals top-ten finalist)

****

Answers for the Mock Bee

Round 1: United States Geography

1. Little Rock
2. Alaska
3. Cape Canaveral
4. Georgia
5. Kansas
6. Georgia
7. Florida
8. Hawaii
9. Lake Ontario
10. Missouri
11. Oregon
12. Oklahoma City
13. Alaska
14. Utah
15. Wisconsin

Round 2: U.S. Cities

1. Vermont
2. Idaho
3. Florida
4. Arizona
5. Pennsylvania
6. New York
7. Oregon
8. South Carolina
9. Georgia
10. Virginia
11. Texas
12. Mississippi
13. South Carolina
14. American Samoa
15. Puerto Rico

Round 3: U.S. City Comparison

1. Amarillo, Texas
2. Shreveport, Louisiana
3. San Diego, California
4. Woods Hole, Massachusetts
5. New Orleans, Louisiana
6. Tucson, Arizona
7. Omaha, Nebraska
8. Syracuse, New York
9. Corpus Christi, Texas
10. Roanoke, Virginia
11. Denver, Colorado
12. Gulfport, Mississippi
13. Canton, Ohio
14. Prudhoe Bay, Alaska
15. Huntington, West Virginia

Round 4: Odd Item Out

1. Mongolia
2. Senegal
3. Russia
4. Uruguay
5. Equatorial Guinea
6. Thailand
7. Saudi Arabia
8. Portugal
9. Mongolia
10. Nigeria
11. Iraq
12. Bangladesh
13. Mozambique
14. Lebanon
15. Nicaragua

Round 5: Continents

1. North America
2. Asia
3. Africa
4. Australia
5. South America
6. South America
7. Asia
8. South America
9. Europe
10. Africa
11. Europe
12. Asia
13. Europe
14. Europe
15. Antarctica

Round 6: World Rivers

1. Loire
2. Zambezi
3. Tagus
4. Tigris
5. Arno
6. Chari
7. Elbe
8. Yellow River
9. Ganges
10. Red River
11. Danube
12. Sava
13. Volga
14. Lena
15. Orinoco

Round 7: Physical Geography

1. Archipelago
2. Sahel
3. Different elevations
4. A strait
5. Core
6. Oasis
7. Opposite directions
8. Mantle
9. Sea-floor spreading
10. Cenozoic
11. Bog
12. Pesticides
13. Brackish water
14. It decreases
15. Occluded Front

Final Round:

1. Number 6, Regina
2. Number 3, Whitehorse
3. Number 5, Iqaluit
4. Number 8, Toronto
5. Number 2, Edmonton
6. Number 7, Winnipeg
7. Number 14, Fredericton
8. Number 11, Charlottetown
9. Number 13, St John's
10. Number 10, Quebec City
11. Number 12, Halifax
12. Number 9, Ottawa
13. Kansas
14. Alabama
15. Vermont
16. Alabama
17. New Jersey

18. Massachusetts
19. Mississippi
20. Maui
21. Minnesota
22. California

Championship Round:

1. Syria
2. Baffin Island
3. Angeles National Forest

Championship Tiebreaker round:

1. Turkey
2. St. Croix
3. Chugach National Forest
4. Lesotho
5. Missouri River
6. Philadelphia

Solutions for Crosswords

State Nicknames

DOWN:

1. Pennsylvania
3. Illinois
4. Oregon
7. South Carolina
8. Minnesota
12. Kansas
13. North Carolina

ACROSS:

2. Missouri
5. New Jersey
6. Indiana
9. Ohio
10. Tennessee
11. New Hampshire
14. Florida
15. Arkansas
16. Utah
17. Massachusetts
18. Rhode Island
19. California
20. Oklahoma

United States, Part II

ACROSS

5. Montana
6. Missouri
10. Ontario

12. California
13. Santa Fe
15. Oregon
16. Maine
17. Washington
19. Mauna Loa

DOWN

1. San Diego
2. Savannah
3. Beaufort
4. New Orleans
6. Michigan
7. Rio Grande
8. Pacific
9. Itasca
11. Oklahoma
14. Oahu
18. Ozark

North American National Parks

ACROSS:

1. Mexico
4. Kluane
6. Sequoia
12. Rio Grande
15. Tula
17. Colorado
18. Channel Islands
19. Panama
20. Alberta

DOWN:

2. Chiapas
3. Jasper
5. Wrangell
7. Ontario
8. Manitoba
9. Yellowstone
10. Nova Scotia
11. Wood Buffalo
13. Crater Lake
14. Yoho
16. Montana

Caribbean Capitals

ACROSS:

2. Port Au Prince
4. Brades
5. Kingstown
8. Bridgetown
10. Managua
11. Roseau
14. San Juan
15. Nassau
16. Tegucigalpa
18. Basseterre
19. Hamilton
20. Port of Spain

DOWN:

1. Belmopan
3. Havana

6. Santo Domingo
7. Oranjestad
9. San Salvador
12. San Jose
13. Kingston
17. Castries

North America, Part II

ACROSS

3. Great Slave
8. Nuuk
9. Quebec
10. Michigan
11. Chihuahua
12. Martinique
13. Alaska
16. Costa Rica
19. Hispaniola

DOWN

1. El Salvador
2. Nicaragua
4. Tehuantepec
5. Bahamas
6. Windward
7. Netherlands
14. Barbados
15. Nova Scotia
17. Trinidad
18. Baffin
19. Haiti

South American Rivers and Regions

ACROSS:

4. Ecuador
5. Equator
6. Chile
7. Patos
12. Parana
14. Guanabara
16. Sao Francisco
17. Orinoco
18. Pantanal

DOWN:

1. Valdes
2. Bolivia
3. Andes
4. Emeralds
7. Pampas
8. Arequipa
9. Paraguay
10. Venezuela
11. Putumayo
13. Patagonia
15. Ucayali

South America, Part II

ACROSS

2. Suriname
6. Montevideo
9. Atlantic

11. Cayenne
12. Sao Paulo
14. Peru
15. Ushuaia
16. Brazil
17. Colombia

DOWN

1. Galapagos
3. MERCOSUR
4. Marajo
5. Titicaca
7. Itaipu
8. Ecuador
9. Argentina
10. Venezuela
13. Chile
14. Pan American
16. Bolivia

Europe

ACROSS

2. Russia
4. Corsica
8. Caspian Sea
9. Julian
10. Edinburg
13. Turkey
14. Black Sea
15. Kola
17. Rotterdam
19. Lithuania
20. Kosovo

DOWN:

1. Islam
3. Iceland
5. Czech Republic
6. Spain
7. Chunnel
11. Isle of Man
12. Palermo
16. Denmark
18. Douro

Europe, Part II

ACROSS

1. Bonifacio
4. Prague
5. Belarus
8. Scotland
10. Danube
11. Elbe
12. Rhone
13. Kiev
16. Bosphorus
18. Crimea
19. Prut
20. Greece

DOWN

2. Finland
3. Jutland
6. Swizerland
7. Balearic

9. Crete
14. Italy
15. Tiber
17. Bosphorus

African Cities

ACROSS:

1. Mombasa
5. Monrovia
6. Djenne
8. Malabo
10. Francistown
12. Lagos
15. Kitwe
16. Benguela
17. Harare
18. Algiers
19. Abidjan

DOWN:

2. Alexandria
3. Johannesburg
4. Kano
6. Dakar
7. Livingstone
9. Addis Ababa
11. Walvis Bay
13. Pretoria
14. Kinshasa

Africa 2, Part II

ACROSS

3. Nigeria
6. Senegal
8. Morocco
10. Kwanza
11. Algeria
12. Ethiopia
14. Mali
15. Mayotte
16. Tanzania
18. Mozambique
19. Namibia

DOWN

1. Praia
2. Cameroon
4. Ghana
5. Mauritania
7. Guinea
8. Malawi
9. Zimbabwe
13. Tunisia
17. Bioko

Asia Landforms

ACROSS:

2. Deccan
4. Ganges
8. Himalayas
9. Arabian

10. Gobi Desert
15. Ural
18. Indus
19. Bay of Bengal
20. Manchuria

DOWN:

1. Persian
3. Thar Desert
5. Siberia
6. Yangtze
7. Lake Balkhash
11. Baikal
12. Sea of Japan
13. Altai
14. Yellow
16. Indian
17. Kunlun

Asia, Part II

ACROSS:

6. Uzbekistan
8. Syria
10. Almaty
11. Ngultrum
12. Oman
13. Japan
14. Afghanistan
17. Sri Lanka
19. Indus

DOWN:

1. Cambodia
2. Turkey
3. Victoria
4. Wakhan
5. India
7. Philippines
9. Yemen
14. Arafura
15. Hainan
16. Eilat
18. Kyrgyzstan

Australia, Antarctica, and Oceania

ACROSS

4. Brisbane
6. Perth
7. Stewart
13. Papua New Guinea
14. Uluru
16. Ronne
18. Antarctica
19. Vinson Massif
20. Tonga

DOWN:

1. Trans Antarctic
2. Tauranga
3. North Island
5. Kakadu
8. Tasmania

9. Kiwi
10. Victoria
11. Tuvalu
12. Coral
15. Yarra
17. Hobart

Australia, Antarctica and Oceania, Part II

ACROSS

1. Wilhelm
4. Roosevelt
5. North
7. New Guinea
12. Apia
14. Carpentaria
18. Tauranga
19. Kiribati
20. Scotia

DOWN

2. Melanesia
3. Foveaux
6. Australia
8. United States
9. Queensland
10. Hawaii
11. New Zealand
13. Mariana
15. Vatu
16. Pacific
17. Tahiti

Physical Geography Terms

ACROSS:

2. Aquifer
5. Abyssal
7. Wind Speed
8. Fold
9. Troposphere
11. Meander
14. Contour
16. Mantle
17. Isobar
18. Eye
19. Delta

DOWN:

1. Humboldt
2. Avalanche
3. Oxbow
4. Cumulonimbus
6. Artesian
10. Igneous
12. Estuary
13. Basalt
15. Crest

Physical Geography, Part II

ACROSS

4. stationary
5. perigee
6. sleet
10. asthenosphere
13. spit

14. loam
15. reg
16. moraine
18. cataract
20. stratosphere

DOWN

1. cirrus
2. Fujita
3. waterspout
7. Santa Ana
8. relief
9. Aeolian
11. shield
12. ebb
17. trench
19. timberline

Cultural Geography

ACROSS

6. Guam
7. Australia
9. Maori
12. Philippines
14. Nigeria
18. Cambodia
20. Portuguese

DOWN

1. Istanbul
2. Denmark
3. Japan
4. Cuba

5. Cyrillic
8. South Africa
10. Russia
11. Spain
13. Triomphe
15. Cowboys
16. Mexico
17. Germany
19. Mecca

Economic Geography

ACROSS

1. MICEX
4. Tin
7. Russia
11. Mesabi
12. Philippines
14. Chile
15. Malaysia
16. Uzbekistan
19. Rwanda
20. WTO

DOWN

2. California
3. Arkansas
5. Oil
6. Jamaica
8. Singapore
9. Pittsburgh
10. Poland
13. South Africa
17. Santos
18. Nauru

Bibliography

Barber, Nicola, Jason Hook, Patricia Levy, Chris Oxlade, and Sean Sheehan. *Question and Answer Encyclopedia: The USA.* New York: Parragon Publishing, 2005.

Bockenhauer, Mark H. *Our Fifty States.* Washington, D.C: National Geographic, 2004.

Britannica Online Encyclopedia. http://www.britannica.com/.

CIA: The World Factbook. https://www/cia.gov/library/publications/the-world-factbook/.

Daily News. http://news.nationalgeographic.com/news/. Accessed September 2009–October 2009.

Ganeri, Anita, Hazel Mary Martell, and Brian Williams. *Encyclopedia of World History.* New York: Parragon Publishing, 2005.

Instructables. http://www.instructables.com/id/Bruschetta-Recipe/.

Lye, Keith. *The New Children's Illustrated Atlas of the World.* Philadelphia: Running Press, Courage Books, 1999.

McNair, Sylvia. *U.S. Territories.* America the Beautiful Second Series. New York: Children's Press, 2001.

Miller, Millie, and Cyndi Nelson. *The United States of America: A State-by-State Guide.* New York: Scholastic, 1999.

National Geographic Society. *National Geographic Student Atlas of the World.* Rev. ed. Washington, DC: National Geographic Society, 2005.

National Geographic Society. *National Geographic United States Atlas for Young Explorers.* Third Edition. Washington, DC: National Geographic Society, 2008.

National Geographic Society. *National Geographic World Atlas for Young Explorers.* Third Edition. Washington, DC: National Geographic Society, 2007.

National Geographic Society. *National Geographic Our World: A Child's First Picture Atlas.* Third Edition. Washington, DC: National Geographic Society, 2006.

Natural Resources Canada, 580 Booth, Ottawa, ON K1A 0E4

Ganeri, Anita. *The Oceans Atlas.* 1st American Edition. New York: Dorling Kindersley, 1994.

GlobalSecurity.org. Alexandria, VA. Accessed October 2009.

Harrison, David L. *Cave Detectives: Unraveling the Mystery of an Ice Age Cave.* San Francisco: Chronicle Books, 2007.

Parks Canada. http://www.pc.gc.ca/eng/index.aspx. Accessed October 2009. 25-7-N Eddy Street, Gatineau, Quebec, Canada, K1A 0M5

Philip, George & Son. *Atlas of the United States.* New York: Oxford University Press, 2006.

Puzzles made at puzzlemaker.discoveryeducation.com.

Sayre, April Pulley. *Wetland.* Tarrytown, NY: Marshall Cavendish, Benchmark Books, 1996.

Sauvain, Philip Arthur. *Rivers and Valleys.* Minneapolis: Carolrhoda Books, 1996.

Sauvain, Philip Arthur. *Oceans.* Minneapolis: Carolrhoda Books, 1996.

Steele, Philip. *Grasslands.* Minneapolis: Carolrhoda Books, 1996.

Sayre, April Pulley. *Temperate Deciduous Forest.* Exploring Earth's Biomes. Minneapolis: Lerner Publications, Twenty-First Century Books, 1994.

Sayre, April Pulley. *Tropical Rain Forest.* Exploring Earth's Biomes. Minneapolis: Lerner Publications, Twenty-First Century Books, 1994.

Sayre, April Pulley. *Tundra.* Exploring Earth's Biomes. Minneapolis: Lerner Publications, Twenty-First Century Books, 2000–2009.

Wilkinson, Philip. *The Kingfisher Student Atlas.* Boston: Kingfisher, 2003.

Wikipedia: The Free Encyclopedia. http://www.wikipedia.org/. Accessed May 2009–May 2011.

About the Author

Ram Iyer is a software engineer working in the Kansas City area. Although he has spent most of his career in the engineering field, his interests extend into the physical sciences, earth sciences, geography, history, world cultures, sports, and political science.

He wrote his first guide, *Geography Bee Demystified*, mainly to help students prepare for the State and the National Geographic Bees. Based on reader responses, he felt there was a need for a second guide that would help budding geographers ease into the rigors of the competition. This guide is a prequel to his first guide that helps a student get prepared for the next level.

Ram and his family live in Olathe, Kansas.

About the Editor

Smitha Gundavajhala is a junior attending Monta Vista High School in Cupertino, California. Smitha loves geography and was a state finalist in the 2009 National Geographic Bee. She placed second in the Scripps Spelling Bee conducted by San Francisco Chronicle in 2009. She placed first in the Spelling Bee in 2007, second in the Vocabulary and Geography Bees in 2009 and first in the Essay Writing Bee in 2011 in other national competitions. She received Outstanding Achievement awards for both Geography and Journalism while at Kennedy Middle School. Smitha is Opinion Editor of her school's publication, El Estoque and is a captain of the Speech Team. Smitha enjoys volunteering in her free time, holding health fairs with Breathe California and working at the HealthTrust Food Basket, and assisting with events in school and around the community with NHS, CSF, Octagon, and Study Buddies. She has participated in several swim competitions with DACA, and has performed classical Indian music and dance around the Bay Area on multiple occasions. Smitha's interests include travel, communications, sciences, and design.

Special thanks
to the following participants who helped me out....

Gentry Clark's love of geography has been the backbone of his education, including his knowledge of history, economics, culture, and human nature. He went to the Texas State Bee four times. Although he didn't quite reach his goal, he came close. He took second place and third place in 2010 and 2011. His interests also include physics, math, martial arts, chess, and music. He has achieved distinctions in Math and Physics competitions. The arts are also a passion for Gentry; he sings and plays lead guitar and keyboard in a home-school rock band in Austin.

Anirudh Kumar is a ninth grade student and an avid Geography enthusiast. His love for Geography started early with exposure to National Geographic magazines and continued through his middle school years. He is a three-time California Geographic Bee state finalist and has won other geography competitions. He is intrigued by the way a single subject can encompass so many strands of life – from weather to geology to economics. His passion for Geography motivates his involvement in contests, contributing to books, helping other interested participants. He aspires to study and make a career in geography.

Omkar Shende is a high school student in the Metro Detroit Area with a vivid interest in math, science and instrumental music. He is very passionate about geography and the world around him. He was a runner up at the National Geographic Michigan State Bee and rank-holder in other national geography competitions. He is a Gold medalist of Midwest Academic Talent Search program. He is also a nationally ranked quiz bowl participant, and has won many awards in academics. He enjoys Model United Nations, which applies many of the skills of geography to everyday issues, and is an award winning delegate.